MORE THAN A DREAM

WILSON SANTOS

More Than A Dream
by Wilson Santos

ISBN: 978-1-937094-72-0

Published by:
Editorial RENUEVO

www.EditorialRenuevo.com
info@EditorialRenuevo.com

Contents

Praise for More than a Dream

It is important to believe in the dream that God has given you, because if you take it for granted, you will never make it come true. However, I also want you to know that just by believing in what God has told you, you will not make that dream become reality.

I encourage you to take some time to read this book, because each one of the tools that Wilson Santos presents in this book is vitally important in order for us to achieve our goals. Although he presents them in a simple, yet profound and practical way. I know they will help you to build a better future.

Rev. Ben Paz
Founder of Words of Life Christian Center
one of the most blessed ministries of New York City

I invite you to spend some time reading a true story that is filled with insights and testimonies that which will serve as tools for you to learn how to dream and how to be ready to demolish everything if necessary, and start again, in order to achieve your dreams.

You have in front of you a book written by a man who is willing to kill his fears in order for the extraordinary to come to light. In my opinion, this story is based on the following words: "Obedience to following God's purpose in your life." Enjoy it to the fullest and put it into practice.

Delki Rosso
Founder and director of House of the Arts Int. School and Ministry
a school of Christian arts

Dedication

Firstly, to God, because He is the reason that I am alive; for thinking of me even before I was born and for loving me unconditionally.

To my grandfather, for being my big hero; he taught me the value of work and self-improvement. Due to the circumstances of his day, he did not go to school, but he always educated himself; he was self-taught. Every person who knew him treated him as a professional.

He built up several business and was an adviser to many others. He was a man with rare wisdom. Only those who knew his story knew that he had not been able to get a college degree.

He easily mastered accounting, literature and history. My grandfather always supported and motivated me to do my best. He believed in education. Having spent part of my childhood with him, I received enough motivation to go to college.

Today my grandfather is not in this world, but he left me a legacy that I pass on to many men of the community that respected him. He always said: "Get education, work hard, rest, and live for your family."

Thank you, grandpa, for departing from this world after leaving me your good advice. Thank you for the time you spent with me. Thank you for always talking to me, and for expecting the best of me.

Acknowledgements

To my God...

Because He is the source of my strength, and the motor of my existence.

To my wife...

For being the person who has been with me during the whole process, always believing the best about me.

To my three children...

They are my treasure and my daily inspiration.

To my parents...

For allowing me to be born and for giving me their best.

To Margarita Vargas...

For treating me like her child, without expecting anything in return.

To Ben Paz...

For supporting me in a moment of darkness, for motivating me to write, for looking me in the eye and telling me, "You can do it."

To Teresa Paz...

For teaching me with her example that one can smile even after having wept.

To Hector and Carol Melo…
More than friends, always unconditional.

To Mandi and Esterlin…
Thank you for your willingness and your words that were filled with power and enthusiasm

To Cesar Garrido…
For your wise words; they have been like water in the desert to me.

To my leaders from ICNY…
For supporting me every single moment.

To the entire leadership team of CCPV…
For taking my family in and giving us so much love. You make us feel special.

To everyone…
Those who have prayed for my happiness, my growth, and who at some point have contributed to my education and personal growth.

Introduction

For years I have heard people talk about success and how to achieve and make your dreams come true, but this work, **MORE THAN A DREAM**, is not only going to help you to be a successful person, but it will also give you the formula for remaining victorious.

The position in which you are now is not the most important thing. The most important thing is the decision you make from this moment on. Your greatness doesn't lie in what you have or possess, but in how ready you are to fight for what you want.

Having failed, ending up in a situation in which your resources have run out, is not part of your defeat. The defeat of every man lies in his lack of vision and persistence. Life is as simple as making a decision and not turning back.

To achieve the things we want is to be willing to suffer for them. These will not come and fall at our feet; nor are they hanging from a tree or found all along the road. It's good that things are this way, because we only learn to value what we have accomplished with great effort and dedication. This is a path that many people want to avoid, but those who dare to walk it are guaranteed success.

Dreams are not fulfilled the day we conceive them, but the day we make them tangible reality; this is the key to the whole process. Not getting things as fast as we would like does not stop us from having them, on the contrary, it makes us value them and prepare ourselves to manage them well. Easy come, easy go; that which quickly appears, quickly vanishes. But everything we are willing to achieve — without leaving the path of patience and perseverance — we will accomplish. And we have to do it in a period of not more than ten years. Only one decade will allow you to see your dreams come true.

Join me in the reading of this book, and when you have read the last page, I guarantee that you will be prepared for something great to happen in your life. If you follow these helpful tips, success is yours; because the information I provide for you in this work — more than what other authors say — about growth, success and dreams, are not only based on academic knowledge, but on what I have found to be true in my own experience. The resources that I offer you here will help you to know how to work the road to success, and what it is you have been lacking so far in order to achieve what you want to accomplish.

So, go ahead, success is waiting for those who will conquer it.

CHAPTER 1

THE PROCESS OF GROWTH

It does not take nine months to make a man; it takes sixty years
André Malraux

The growth of everything that is alive is a process. We can't achieve the things we want in one day. There are people who tell me: "Say it and it will be done," and although that can be true in regards to faith and visualization, it has nothing to do with the real process, because everything on earth has to undergo a process and you cannot avoid it.

Someone said to me: "Wilson, why can't people, through faith, achieve all they want at once?" That is easy to answer. If you analyze the law of nature, you will see that every living thing is born, grows, reproduces and dies. It's that simple. It's just the nature of things. And if you don't like it, you will have to make a planet for yourself alone, the way you want it.

This is a law that was established from the beginning of the universe, a law that was created in parallel with the creation of living things. This law shows that everything is a process. I have seen highly skilled people, with talent and intelligence, who never get anywhere, and that's because they don't want to go through the process of growth. You, however, can achieve everything you want in life, as long as you understand the power of letting yourself undergo and complete the natural process.

I have seen highly skilled people, with talent and intelligence, who never get anywhere, and that's because they don't want to go through the process of growth.

The river has its own natural course, therefore, water doesn't have to make any effort to run along it; water follows the course of the stream. In life, the course or channel is formed by the process, therefore, go with the flow and you will reach your destination.

Allow the person you chose to be your mentor — or your boss — to guide you. That premise is very important to reaching the goal you have set. Those who think they know the way to perfection have very serious problems.

False expectations yield false results

While talking to a young girl who attended a seminar with me, I asked her if she would like to earn money. Her answer was that she didn't need it. "How is that?" I asked her. "I have plenty of money," she stated with certainty. I looked at her, and saw that the way she spoke and dressed was not that of a wealthy person, nor even close to one. I was able to infer that the young girl was speaking a lot about declarations, but not about the process.

That's how I concluded that she didn't have money in her bank account. She was exaggerating and acting unrealistically. Why? Because she was declaring herself in abundance and yet, she didn't want to know how to earn money; which undoubtedly, I knew she needed. To earn money you have to know its laws. No matter how many times you declare yourself in abundance, if you don't go through the process, you will not obtain it, unless you are a fan of gambling and hit the jackpot, which is a very unlikely possibility. I advise you not to take that path.

No matter how many times you declare yourself in abundance, if you don't go through the process, you will not obtain it.

I have always heard that for many people declarations have power; that words create everything; but what I believe words do is they originate everything. The process is what brings it to perfection. Where does the process originate? In your thoughts, in your words, in your actions, in your habits, in your character, and ends in destiny which is the result of what you have forged.

Let God take you on the right path, but don't forget that life is very mischievous; it will always try to trip you up so you fall. If you don't have the right expectations, you will fall and will never be able to get up.

When life asks you, "Will you quit or keep on?" always answer, "I'm going to keep on keeping on."

When I was little, my grandmother was in charge of my religious education. She taught me that God made everything out of nothing. I would ask her, "What is nothing?" And she would answer, "Nothing is nothing." Today, as a result of my own investigation, I have come to know that that is not true. Things do not come from nothing, but instead they come from things that were unseen (as it says in Hebrews 11:3). There is a big difference. Things unseen means that even though everything existed in the mind of the Eternal One, it was not manifested in the universe. Those who speak about evolution don't like this thought.

As for me, I have never seen a monkey become a man. But I have seen many things that didn't exist, become real before men's eyes. What am I saying? I am saying that everything you can see today at some point in the past was not seen, and the reason you can see it today is because it has gone thought the process that brought it into existence. All the things you can see are things that came by means of this process: 1) an idea, 2) a word, 3) an action, 4) a habit, 5) a character, 6) a destiny.

Therefore, when we don't believe in the process of creation, we fail to look at things from the standpoint of reality and logic. Everything out there — buildings, roads, medicine, inventions, etc. — already existed, even though it wasn't seen. However, it started to be seen when the idea popped into someone's brain because of the ability given them by their Creator, and it was incorporated into the process that would make it materialize and exist. Things do not evolve on their own, they need to be created.

Everything starts in the human mind

Everything you see on this earth started in a mind, the mind of the Eternal One. And our mind united to His is omnipresent, omniscient, omnipotent, qualities that are divine in themselves and in which men can be like God. Now, we cannot dispute the fact that we are similar to God only in our mind; (for it is the mind that keeps all that is eternal and indestructible, such as love, character, soul, conscience, thoughts, etc.).

Robert Stone stated that after studying the human mind, he found the following phenomena:

- People who could remember texts and complete books having read them only one time.

- People who were able to find mineral veins, underground water reservoirs or oil deposits, using a pendulum over a map.

- Men and women endowed with the ability to see the future and see with complete certainty events that were happening.

- Individuals who were capable of curing sick people with their hands, even of diseases that were considered incurable in the medical field.

- Individuals who inexplicably always sensed ways to attract money and material success in almost any activity that they initiated.

- People whose presence radiated an aura of well-being, friendliness and a feeling of safety to all those who were around them. Charismatic people to a superlative degree.

- Specialists in mental calculations, mathematical advances and exact sciences.

- People with the ability to influence others mentally, by subduing the will of others quickly and silently.

- Beings endowed with the ability to move objects from a distance, bending metals or bursting glass.

- Men and women of normal appearance, but with extraordinary physical strength, with great endurance and inexhaustible energy.

- People who could see what was happening at a distance while closing their eyes and concentrating for a few seconds.

- Gifted beings that cooperated with the police on a regular basis to solve crimes, concentrating on the belongings of the victims or the perpetrators.

- People who could predict with amazing accuracy the movements of stock markets, and who were employed by financial institutions to earn lots of money.

- Uneducated men who were able to see the human energy field, accurately diagnose diseases, and even hit on highly effective treatments.

Those of us who are believers and have seen these phenomena know that they have their sources, sometimes positive and other times negative, but the point here is not to analyze the source, but to tell you that no matter what your beliefs are, (because we all believe in something, even those who say they don't believe): we cannot deny that our mind is the reception center of everything that happens to us and everything we do.

Everything starts with an idea

The human mind is the greatest creation there is in the universe. Those who have studied it state that human beings barely use 10% of its capacity; even the most remarkable man who has lived on the planet does not exceed that percentage. On the other hand, no machine is able to do what the mind can achieve. It is said that, to make a machine with the power of the human mind, even with all the technology of the modern world, it would have to be made as big as a ten-story building and even then it would still have a very important deficiency: it would not be able to create one single thought.

That is what makes the difference between men and robots, because all the other living things and machines that exist are incapable of producing a single thought. Only man can produce thoughts without limit; there is no limit for him. And that is what makes us similar to the Creator. Hence, it is possible that while I am writing, at some moment my ideas may go away. But when that happens, the only thing I do is close my eyes and connect with Him again and my ideas clearly come back to me.

Only man can produce thoughts without limit;
there is no limit for him.

It is important that each day we have a quiet time to connect with the infinite source. I want to assure you that if you remain in deep quietude and complete solitude for only ten minutes, it will make your body relax and your brain work through its neurons, so that they create new thoughts and ideas. The Teacher used to spend time in the mountains every day, thinking in deep solitude and in an attitude of constant meditation. *(John 6:15)*

Ideas are like powerful lightning bolts that come from the Eternal One to your brain. If you don't make them tangible reality and develop them, they go back and others take advantage of them. That happens to all of us. I have had ideas and projects — to which I have even assigned names — but which I have not brought into reality; later on I have found other people who have developed them and even given them the same name. My wife, for instance, always told me she wanted to develop a television program for women. She gave me the name, the script, the objective — she told me everything about the project. But whenever I encouraged her to come out on my show with a segment of hers, she told me she was not ready.

One day, I was invited to participate in someone else's show, and to my utter astonishment, that person was developing a presentation with the exact ideas that my wife had expressed to me. My jaw dropped. The strangest thing is that it even had the same name as the one my wife had mentioned.

So when you have an idea and don't put it into practice, it will go away, and another person will bring it to reality and develop it. Even if they are brilliant ideas, if you don't put them into action, you will lose them and only be left thinking and saying: "I had the same idea". Nevertheless, the saddest thing is that it will not add to your bank account or to your personal satisfaction or spiritual growth.

It does not matter how significant an idea is, if it stays in our mind, it does not have any value. Ideas only take on value when they are put into practice. Ideas without action are a dime a dozen. But if you act in accord with them, one single idea can change your destiny. Every great company, church, business, country, fortune or invention started with an idea that someone turned from a noun into a verb, in other words, from idea to action.

Ideas only take on value when they are put into practice.

Many people are happy when an idea comes to their mind, and they say: "Wow, a light went on in my head." However, the only person who has made money for turning on a light bulb was Thomas Edison, its inventor, and it worked for him because he dared to get it out of his mind and put it into existence. He invented it. Historians say that he had to try ten thousand times until he got it right.

What I'm trying to tell you with all of this is to take advantage of the power of every idea, to recognize that they are gifts from God; therefore, do not waste them. Always carry with you a recorder, a notebook to take notes, so that, when you wake up in the night startled by a thought, you can even take advantage of those night ideas. Ideas that are brought into tangible reality are guaranteed to grow. Don't leave the opportunity to take advantage of them for later; pay attention to them and you will see how they start to grow.

Words become actions

Words have power to create things. In the Bible we find a very significant statement, which says that "the word was God". But when we observe the process, we can not only see that words were used in creation, but that there was also an action that gave shape to those words; because in the account of creation, it says that the Holy

Spirit moved over the face of the waters. The Spirit was the force that gave power to the words.

Words can only create something when there is an intermediate force that gives them form through movement. We see an example of this when the idea of owning a house enters a person's mind. He communicates the idea to his friends, and to everyone who comes across his path. He wants a house (statement), he even draws a picture of it in his head (visualization), however, the house will not appear unless there is an intermediate force to bring it to concrete action and cause the building to be built.

Words can only create something when there is an intermediate force that gives them form through movement

---

Words are not enough; there must be a power that brings them to reality, a force that incubates them. In essence, words contain nothing; they just reveal something. Many people think that by saying positive words, positive things will happen, but that will not occur, unless there is a force that propels them. That force makes words reveal things to you; but the realization or accomplishment — putting them into action and making them reality — that depends on the movement produced by the force that accompanies that word.

I have seen people with many dreams; they dream a lot; they spend their life dreaming, but few of those dreams become reality; and the reason is that most of their dreams remain on a piece of paper or in their minds. Of course, it is important that everything we are going to do be written down somewhere, and that we plan everything we want. But for them to just be ideas on a piece of paper that will never turn into reality, is another matter. You should add details to the plans you have and write them down; that is the platform for great action. But once you write them down, if you file them away, that file will become the coffin for your ideas, and will prevent you from having what you want so much.

I knew a great man, an intelligent guy who was well connected to the source of revelation and wisdom (God). Despite his abilities, he had a hard time making decisions. That led him to be such a fearful person that he rarely turns an idea into action. Now, it is important to be aware that the balance point between the process and growth, is for our ideas and words to become actions. We must always keep this in mind: Good ideas = good actions. Good actions = good results.

Remember that every decision you make in the present will become your future. A drama that helped me understand the power of decisions was that of a man who liked to mess with women's feelings. His game reached its lowest point when he married two women and took them to live in the same house. He saw that as something normal, while the two women tried to get used to it and to cope with their new environment.

In their desperation, the two women became friends and began to discover that between them there was an attraction that was more than just friendship. The two women began to sense that they felt a physical attraction between them. (That usually happens when two people get confused in regards to their sexuality because they are abused by someone of the opposite sex.) So they became lovers; which, of course, started causing problems for the man who thought of himself as a Casanova. The relationship was in danger because he couldn't bring happiness to the two women who for so long had endured his abuse and humiliations.

Now the two women slept together and they didn't allow him to touch them. That worried him even more because, even though he was supporting two women, he did not have either. Until the day came that the man demanded that the women tell him the reason for their behavior. When they told him the truth, the man — angered — asked them to leave the house. To which they replied that they were not leaving, since one of them was pregnant with his child, and, if he insisted on kicking them out of the house, they were going to turn him in for polygamy. The man didn't have any other option but to leave the house.

Time went by, the child was born and the two women took care of all his needs. One day, when the two women took a walk to the park with the child, the child went a little ways away from his mother; neither of them realized that the father of the child was watching him at a distance, and he took advantage of the opportunity, approached the child and when he was with him he asked:

"Who are those two women that are with you?"

The child responded:

"My aunt and my mother."

Then the man asked:

"Don't you miss your father?"

To which the child answered:

"No, because my aunt and my mother love me and they take care of all my needs."

The mother, who at last saw the boy from afar talking to a stranger, called him. The child very kindly said goodbye, while the father, with tears in his eyes, found himself alone, and a feeling of sadness overwhelmed his soul. His best friend, who accompanied him and was watching the scene, came up to him, embraced him and told him:

"Buddy, I told you that whoever plays with fire ends up getting burned."

With this narration I want to highlight three important things in regard to decisions:

1. Life doesn't only depend on the decisions that are made, rather, it depends on good decisions.

   We can't go through life doing everything that comes to our mind, and much less, hurting people with our actions. Therefore, make sure that every time you make a decision, it is for the common good.

2.   All your choices mark your future and the future of others.

It is important to consider what we do, how we do it and why we do it. The purpose of everything we do makes a difference. That is why it is important that we ask questions of ourselves, to see what are the intentions that motivate us.

3.   Every action causes a reaction.

What goes around comes around. If you get used to pursuing your growth and happiness at the expense of the misfortune of others, you will ride up on a wave that will give you momentary success, but it will make you crash at any time, when you least expect it.

There is a song that makes me think a lot; the lyrics go like this: "You chose your path and that is your destiny forever". The consequences of your decisions can stay with you the rest of your life, for better or for worse.

When I was going through adolescence, I had a friend who married a guy without loving him. She married him with the sole purpose of punishing her ex boyfriend. They would kiss in front of him; they would be affectionate to the extreme, but only to punish him. However, the only person who was punished in the end, was her. She was unable to be happy and was sick most of the time.

The consequences of your decisions can stay with you your whole life.

You can't do something and not expect a reaction, whether good or bad. My friend's life was never the same again. You can mend the bad actions from the past by making good decisions in the present, but you will never be able to change them; you already made them and the effect is what you are today. That is why I want you to focus on your present and not on the actions of the past, because the actions of the past are your present, but the actions of the present will be your future.

So, if you are happy with your present, keep doing what you have been doing. But if you feel that something is missing; that there is an emptiness within you, that you don't have everything you want, you need to make a change. Changes are painful, but are the only thing that guarantees different results. The strange thing is that many people who keep doing the same thing would like to have different results, but that is not possible.

Most people remain in their comfort zone. They would love to grow and they even dream about doing so, but they want to do it without putting anything at risk. Nevertheless, it is impossible to take a step forward without taking a risk. Every time you advance, you are taking a risk. And that's because every action is accompanied by a risk. Whenever you feel the desire to improve yourself, to do something more than what you already have done, remember that you have to be willing to take risks. But it is also important to know that you can reduce the level of risk if you take the right steps.

In conclusion, what I am saying in this chapter is that, in order for a person to get where he has resolved and reach his goals, he has to learn to cross the river of process. Therefore, if you want to finish something, first you have to start it. If you want to graduate from the university, begin by enrolling, don't try to avoid the process; on the contrary, enjoy it.

Never think that if you put something in your mind today, you will find it tomorrow showing up in your bank account, your family, your health, your business or your church. Everything is a process and you must learn to go through it.

CHAPTER 2

THE HABIT OF BEING HAPPY

Human happiness is usually not achieved with great strokes of luck, which may rarely occur, but with little things that happen every day.
Benjamin Franklin

All humans are forged by habits. Habits are what shape our character. What do I mean by that? That all our actions become habits and these habits are what rule our lives. I would define habits as actions that are automatic or done as conditioned responses.

A habit is an action that is repeated constantly or periodically by a person, whether consciously or unconsciously. Habits, more than any other thing, define us as people; that is to say, the person that you are in the present is a direct result of your present habits. A relevant example is that of boxers. They have the ability to dodge blows without thinking; they do it just by reflexes. A boxer throws a punch and bobs, throws a punch and bobs.

We can compare that to life. You are a boxer and the adversities of life are your opponent. Even though you know that there are adversities in life, they don't decide your future; rather, they are your training. Like the boxer who has to train a lot, every single day, even when he is on vacation. Even though he doesn't have a fight pending, the good boxer doesn't leave his training to the moment of the fight. On the contrary, he trains all the time and on a regular basis.

Likewise we have to train ourselves to live. We don't live just for the sake of living, but to win in life, because we didn't come into the world to be losers, but to be champions, to be winners. Therefore, we can't live bitter, grumpy, full of hard feelings and resentment; that is not a good life. God wants you to be happy, and of course, you also want to be happy even though you don't know how.

Happiness is the most sought-after feeling. Why? Because

there is no point in having a lot of money and possessions and everything else if in the end you're not happy.

We have to train ourselves to live ... because we didn't come into the world to be losers, but to be champions, to be winners.

While I was an evangelistic pastor and had my television program on NBC in Spanish, better known as Telemundo, I had the experience of dealing with a family that was going through a difficult situation. A man with a wife and three children decided to be happy with another woman. But it didn't turn out the way he imagined it would. The mistress got pregnant with his child, and the child was born with Down's syndrome. The man began to suffer from terrible depression and with a bitter sense of guilt that made him feel miserable and full of destructive feelings.

He was at a crossroads; on the one hand, he wanted to go back to his wife and family; on the other, the idea of abandoning his sick child weighed him down. This situation lasted one year, until one day he decided to go back home. Nevertheless, tranquility didn't return with him. When a person doesn't take into account the things that can take away his happiness and what keeps him from being happy, he will hurt himself and all those around him.

When a person doesn't take into account the things that can take away his happiness and what keeps him from being happy, he will hurt himself and all those around him.

I still remember when a friend called me and told me: "Wilson, if you are not in the place you're supposed to be, and doing what you're supposed to do, you and your loved ones are in danger." The man with the two women went back to his house, but he was confused, sick, depressed; meanwhile, on the other hand, he had the mistress making him feel guilty. Finally, he ended up taking his life.

Why do I tell you this story? Because the point I want to make with you is that you should form habits that make you happy, because most people have formed habits that make them unhappy. Why? Because they repeat to themselves the negative things so many times that, in the end, they become negative people. There are people who have the habit of getting depressed, criticizing, hating, feeling guilty, and punishing themselves.

Negative thinking is a bad habit. Having thoughts like the ones we mentioned above creates very dangerous habits. Thoughts are like a spring that gives birth to a flowing river. And bad thoughts, like other kinds of thoughts, start like small drops dripping from rocks; they gain strength as they go along and drag everything in their path, forming a great current that goes all the way to the ocean.

Our thoughts are like drops of water dripping, our mind is the channel through which our thoughts pass, and the ocean is our body. Why? Because we are the result of what we think. If our thoughts are dirty and contaminated, our entire body will be dirty and the people who get close to us will end up sick, infected and contaminated. No one wants to bathe in a dirty ocean. When I go from New York to Pennsylvania, I have to go through New Jersey; it always catches my attention that the lakes in New Jersey have a bad smell. I ask myself why — even thought they look so pretty — they have such a bad smell. The reason is obvious: it is because the water doesn't flow; it is stagnant.

Our habits begin with ideas that become actions until they become part of our existence. If we have the habit of not letting our thoughts flow out, and today we repeat the same thoughts we had yesterday, we will be forming mental lakes instead of rivers, which then will pollute our body and our character. It is said that humans process 60,000 thoughts a day; the problem is that the common man processes today the same thoughts he had yesterday, and the day before, and so on. He will process the same thoughts tomorrow.

Where do habits begin? Habits begin when we turn our ideas into actions until they become part of our existence. I remember when I bought my first car. It was in the country where I was born. I felt very proud of having been able to do so. Although the car was seven years old, and was of a brand I had never heard of before, I was happy because it had been my childhood dream. It was a dream come true. But, where or what did this dream come from?

I remember that when I went to school I didn't wear shoes, and I always wore shorts. Since the school was four miles away from my house, I put out a lot of effort because I had to walk. Now, when I think about those times, I realize that it was in those moments when I was walking to school that I had the wonderful idea of buying a Volkswagen some day; in particular, I wanted a Beetle. The reason why I purposed this for myself was the following. One rainy day when I was going to school, the engineer who was building the school drove by and splashed my clothing with mud. His car was a Volkswagen.

However, the first car I bought was not a Volkswagen, but a Yugo. The funny thing is that it didn't take very long for me to find out that my car lived up to its name to the maximum. It was a real yugo (Spanish for yoke), but I was happy because no one in my family or my close relatives had been able to own a car; I was the only one to achieve that. Nevertheless, why wasn't my car of the brand I had purposed to get? Because as time goes by, dreams that are not well-defined vanish, and we end up accepting whatever life gives us, not what we really want. That is the reason why we always need to ask our inner being what it is we really want.

As time goes by, dreams that are not well-defined vanish; and we end up accepting whatever life gives us.

When I bought my fancy Yugo, I didn't know anything about cars. The worst thing was that I didn't even know how to drive it. I always had to employ a friend of mine to drive it for me, and the only thing I did was go to the university, which was located some forty miles away. However, I think that the lack of a weekly check, the long and tedious wait, besides the "yoke" which that responsibility became, took away the enthusiasm of my friend; so he decided to find something else to do.

I found out about his decision one day when it was time for us to leave and he didn't show up. I called him on the phone and he told me he was not able to go with me that day. At that point I panicked, but since I didn't have many options, I decided to drive the car myself. Now, the thing was that I didn't have a license and I had never received any driving lessons; the only thing I knew was that, if I wanted to get to the university that day, I had to drive the car myself. So I took the wheel in my hands, and my legs started to shake at that moment. Immediately I felt like I was committing suicide. I did not understand anything, and to make matters worse, the car was standard, not automatic.

I tried to start the car and instead of adjusting the side rearview mirrors to look back, I adjusted them to look at the pavement. The reason for that was that I thought I could guide myself with the white stripes and because I had to change gears manually, it seemed impossible to me to perform such a feat. Imagine, I had to step on the clutch, move the shift lever, hold the steering wheel, speed up, stop the car if necessary, and I had to do it all at the same timeas I had to calculate the distance between my vehicle and the vehicles around me, be alert for unforeseen circumstances that may occur and — on top of that — be careful that a police office wouldn't pull me over and catch me driving without the proper documents. What an awful mess.

Amid the earnest intentions, I felt so frustrated that I thought I would never be able to learn to drive, but as they say in my country, "necessity has the look of a terrorist" (necessity can justify a person's trying desperate things); that is why I had to keep trying. That day I arrived at the university, white as a sheet; I looked like death warmed over. All my classmates asked what had happened, because I would ask permission to go to the bathroom every half hour. The stress had gone to my stomach. That day I missed the last two classes because I made sure I left early to avoid the night overtaking me on the road. Nevertheless, I kept on trying, practicing and driving to the university until I managed to do it naturally. I did everything without thinking or trying hard. I could pass another car without any effort. I could drive with only one hand, move the shift lever, eat something and even admire the landscape, and I could do all those things at the same time. Phenomenal!

What happened? I practiced so many times that what seemed impossible before turned into a habit, and once it had become a habit, it became routine. That's how it is; habits are created with practice; that's why it's so important what we do today, because our future depends on it. How are habits formed? Habits are created when we repeat an action seven times a day for more than twenty-one days. But remember that this also includes words which — even though they don't create things on their own — trigger events, and these in turn unleash creative action.

Habits are created with practice.

In the Bible we find this fact when it says: "In the beginning was the Word, and the Word was with God, and the Word was God". *(John 1:1 KJV)* We also find it on one occasion when a centurion addressed Jesus to ask him to heal his servant, and told him: "Therefore I did not even think myself worthy to come to You. But say the word, and my servant will be healed." *(Luke 7:7 NKJV)*. This man knew that one word pronounced by Jesus would be enough for his servant to be healed.

Where words come from

Words are the result of thoughts. That is why I always say that as your thoughts are, so shall your words be; as your words are, so shall your actions be, and as your actions are, so shall be your habits be. In order to change your habits, you must modify your way of thinking, and you have to train yourself to do that. The hatred that is in your heart does not disappear just because you want it to; you have to work at it, you have to train yourself.

Love and forgiveness should be habits; otherwise, life will be an uphill climb. From childhood we are formed with bad habits, which are within us and we don't even realize it. We need to work on these, starting with our thoughts. If our thoughts are transformed, our lives will be also. As are the thoughts of a man, so is he. Thoughts take shape with our words; this is something that I will explain in greater detail later.

Character and Personality

People have tried to define character down through the years, but one of the most accurate concepts is the one that says: "Character is the hallmark that identifies us and makes us different from our fellow man; it's the result of social learning." That leads us to understand that we are unique and that we have an exclusive set of reactions and habitual behaviors that we have acquired over the course of our lives.

Character is the unique identity that every human being has; it isn't transferred, nor inherited; it is forged through circumstances, thoughts, decisions, cultures and the underlying events of the individual. Every action that a man performs and that takes place around him, contributes to the formation of his character. That's why there are no two people alike in the universe, although they may have the same physique.

> *Character is the unique identity that every human being has; it isn't transferred, nor inherited; it is forged through circumstances, thoughts, decisions, cultures and the underlying events of the individual.*

Many people confuse character with personality and temperaments. However, character and personality are two different things. The question we should ask ourselves is: What is personality? It is the appearance of a person, it is what you see of a woman or a man. Scripture puts it this way: "But the Lord said to Samuel: 'Don't look at his appearance or at his physical stature, because I have refused him, for the Lord does not sees as man sees; for man looks at the outward appearance, but the Lord looks at the heart." *(1 Samuel 16:7 NKJV)*

When we see a person who smiles, we may believe that they are a friendly, cheerful, dynamic person; but when we see someone with a tense face, we might think that that person is unfriendly or short-tempered. Besides, the expression on our face, our dress, our hairstyle, our way of walking, etc., leaves an impression on others, whether good or bad, especially when we are in front of people who don't know us.

When I began selling books — a job that I started in order to attend school (later on I will tell more about this subject) — it was very difficult for me to move forward in the profession, because I am a shy person, and since I come from a home made up of very poor people, I was scared to talk to economically well-off people. That made me the worst salesman under the sun. I only entered places where people looked like myself or a little better than myself. It must be noted that this behavior is most natural, since people attract others who think like them. They are like magnets; everything that comes around them along their way sticks to them.

Believe it or not, appearance has great power over people — over us and over others. But, we cannot fall into the permanent error of believing that we can cover our flaws with mere makeup. We should also learn to grow entirely; that is, both internally and externally; and in every aspect of our life. The plan of the Eternal One is that we grow physically, mentally, materially, economically and spiritually. One of the closest friends of Jesus said it to you very well: "Beloved, I pray that you may prosper in all things and be in health, just as your soul prospers." *(3 John 1:2 NKJV)*

As I have pointed out, I was very shy, I had low self-esteem, and that's why my life was an uphill struggle. I was going from bad to worse, as if I were being paid a salary to encourage the needy. Many times I came out of houses wiping my tears away. The reason is that I met people who had more problems than myself and their stories caused me much pain. It was then that I finally learned the power of personality. So, I took a class to learn how to greet, how to smile, how to knock on a door, how to dress, how to stand, how to talk, how to comb my hair, etc.

During the summer, for instance, when I went out to sell, my supervisors would send me to a town that was far from home, and they would put me up in any place except a hotel. Almost always it was a house with a group of strangers who were in the same situation as myself. We would sleep on the floor with the mice as our best companions. That's why we grew very fond of rats for being such faithful companions. I remember that on many occasions I didn't eat all day, and most of the time it wasn't because I didn't have money, but because it wasn't very comforting to know that if you were to buy something, you had to share it with all those that were with you, and, since all felt the same way, no one bought any food.

Other times we didn't eat because there was no money, but we stayed there with the assurance that our director — who now had a nice office — had gone through the same difficulties as we were and had achieved his dream. My motto was always: "If he could, I can." I have always been inspired by people who have achieved success in the same area where I aim to succeed. There are people who come into situations wanting to teach the ones who are already there. Such people have many difficulties; I prefer to learn from those who have already arrived, although that doesn't mean doing all that they have done, because that doesn't work, either; I have to take them as a source of inspiration.

Two years went by like this without success, but,

after taking a one-week seminar with Doctor Milton Presentation, everything changed. This man, instead of focusing his seminar on how to sell something to someone, focused on how to sell ourselves and how to change our self-image. I have always heard about how to sell, and the importance of making a good presentation of the product for the client, but I had not heard about the importance of making a good presentation of oneself.

When I found out that I had to make a good presentation of myself, I told the directors in the office that I would work that year if they would place me in a decent house, one that would make me feel proud instead of making me feel like a sardine in a can. At first they didn't even consider it, but I made so many promises that I ended up convincing them. It was the assurance with which I spoke that caused them to see me in a different way. Being confident of ourselves and what we do is the key that God has placed in our hands to open all the doors of success. Jesus said to him: "If you can believe, all things are possible to him who believes." *(Mark 9:23 NKJV)* Living in a positive way, loving, and believing is the key that releases everything.

The director didn't promise me anything, but said he was going to try, and for me, that was enough. I knew that my faith was triggering everything. I was determined to experience a change; I wanted a different summer, and to go back home with a triumphant smile. I was so confident, that I began to prepare immediately to achieve it. So I called my cousin Joselito, in the United States, and I asked him to send me a thousand Dominican pesos (equivalent to seventy-five dollars), with which I bought a new briefcase (an executive briefcase) and some shoes.

The time came to start working, and the director took me in his car to the place where I was going to live. I was surprised by the fact that he took me to a two-story house, where there were two cars in the garage, a maid, and a beautiful elderly couple who lived in United States, but who were in the country enjoying their house. Mrs. Silvia and Mr. Lino treated me as if they were my parents. When I arrived at their house, they took me out for a ride around the city in their Jipeta (luxury car in the Dominican Republic, in other countries they called them "trocas" (pickup trucks), but they are nothing but luxury off-road vehicles).

That new house and the comfort that Mr. Lino and Mrs. Silvia offered me, made my life expectations change even more. That made the concept that I had of myself change for the better. If you work hard, try to enjoy life, to eat, to dress and rest well; take time to do fun things with your loved ones, and live in a comfortable place, and that — in its turn — will give you new strength to work. Many people work more than eight hours a day, but they don't take time to enjoy what they earn with their hard work.

That summer I became the Og Mandino of the Dominican Republic, a champion of sales, and I went back to the university to live like a son of a king. The interesting thing was that the following summer I went from being a sales person to a director. So what happened to me? I changed the thoughts I had about myself. The failures we have in life have nothing to do with what people think of us; they only have to do with what we think of ourselves.

Failures ... only have to do with what we think of ourselves.

Happiness isn't something we can obtain by changing our way of smiling, but we can start there. What I mean to say is that, when you smile, dress, and walk like a happy person, with time, you will become a happy person.

People see what I project

What people think of me is — in most cases — merely the image I project. Of course, I don't mean that we have to try to please others; we must have a healthy balance. Many people, by trying to please others, are left without their personalities. You also have to remember that it isn't possible to please everyone, but it is very important to know how most other people feel, because it's possible that many don't feel the same way.

My argument, however, is that if we carefully analyze the lives of those who have wanted to change the world, we have to see that their lives have been spent in adverse circumstances. While seemingly, most people have rejected their ideals, the reality is that, afterward, the fact that they have had massive support makes it clear that their ideals were good, noble, praiseworthy. But in spite of that, some external force, of whatever nature — political, religious, etc. — made people reject them.

That is because free expression — whether of spoken words or actions and emotions — is misunderstood and misused, because even in countries with more freedom, people are still enslaved by fear, poverty, collective opinions, and the prejudices that prevail in their communities. It is very important, for people who want to achieve success, to follow common sense, but not common dreams; that is, if you want to grow, you have to take into account what it is that people need, not what you need.

With this, what I want to emphasize is that personality is very important when we present ourselves to the outside world. In my experience, working with people and doing public speaking, which I have been doing for more than 17 years, I have proved that a good presentation, clothing, a smile, etc., opens even the most difficult door. A smile softens even the hardest heart, and a good presentation of oneself leads us to what seems impossible to achieve. As they say: "There will never be a second opportunity to make a good first impression."

When I learned the value of a good presentation, I asked Mr. Lino to lend me his car keys and I always carried them with me; of course, only the keys, not the car. Every time I had to go to a house, office, or any other place, I would stop, clean the sweat off my face, get the keys out, and then enter swinging them in my hands. That opened countless doors that would not have opened otherwise. Of course, at this point in life, I would not advise anyone to do that. I did it at that time due to my lack of experience.

Therefore, personality is what you project, and doesn't

necessarily have to be real, or what you are experiencing at that moment. In a motivational CD by Mr. Alex Day, I heard a phrase I liked: "Start by pretending, end up believing." People who allow themselves to be carried away by their feelings find it hard to achieve what they want, since their feelings go up and down, no matter who the person is, where he was born, or how much money he has in his bank account. The law of emotions is for all; the difference is that some people have control over their feelings, while the rest are controlled by them.

> *Some people have control over their feelings, while the rest are controlled by them.*

Personality is what is seen, and the only thing people will know about you. That is why it is so important that we don't externalize our emotions beyond our inner circles such as our family, church, and other support groups. It's possible that many people are asking, "Isn't that hypocrisy?" I would not call it that, because hypocrisy is what is hidden in order to deceive, something we exhibit for the purpose of deceiving, not growing. Since the hypocrite has no faith in himself, he deceives, because he believes that things will not come true otherwise.

Personality is something that you sustain, cherish and externalize. Even though at some point you may think you don't have it, you use it to be what you want to be. Personality is something real even when it is something external. On the other hand, hypocrisy is based on things that are not real and will never exist. Personality is what people see of you, which is very valuable to them. The beginning of change is based on personality, as you begin to project what you want to be. Personality is an attitude, not a delusion, because you talk, walk, and act like the person you want to be and will become.

It is a matter of disciplining yourself, believing it and practicing it until it happens, that is what I'm talking about. What do I want you to know? That personality is a cover letter. Next time you want a change in life, start with your personality.

A happy person isn't only the one who feels complete inside, but the one who also shows it on the outside. Putting on a good face makes us grow and become liked by other people. Also, it opens doors to new dimensions; physical, mental, and spiritual dimensions. Your future starts with the formation of a habit, and this begins with a good personality; but good personality begins with a good attitude.

In conclusion, I think that to be happy is to make the decision to be happy, it isn't something that is left to chance. What's more, it has to do with the attitude we take on, with the desire we cultivate, with the smile we show, with the face we change, everything starts there. That's why when a man and a woman decide to live better, they have to work at it. Showing people your best face will give you a better life. Many people say: "I live the way I want to live." These people will indeed live, but with many problems; and they will face situations that they could have avoided. This is the power of what they show with their actions. Many of them are not bad people, but their actions make them look like they are.

CHAPTER 3

TEMPERAMENTS, CHARACTER AND DESTINY

Temperament often determines the value of men.
François de La Rochefoucauld

The Temperaments

The word temperament comes from the Latin term *temperamentum*, which means "mixture in the right proportion" that is, moderation. Temperament refers to the state of mind, the ability to adapt, the intensity, the level of activity and regularity. For many psychologists, temperament is related to the nervous system of the individual. Nevertheless, temperaments are genetic traits that are related to our past and are inherited from our parents and grandparents, among others. Therefore, you don't have to do anything to get yours; it comes in the same wrapper as you.

All human beings have a combination of at least two or three temperaments. According to Hippocrates, who existed four centuries before Christ, the temperaments are divided into: sanguine, choleric, melancholic and phlegmatic. Later we will talk about this in detail. Meanwhile the only thing we will highlight is that there is a big difference between character, temperament, and personality.

There are people who think that if they have a difficult temperament, they have a bad character, or vice-versa. Your temperament is not your character, although it is part of it. No one can choose the temperament he will be born with or the one he would most like to have now.

Character

Character is the combination of personality and temperament. Character can't be faked because it's what we really are. You can't dress it in different clothes;

neither can you change it by putting on a happy face. En the Bible, character receives the name of "old man," and "new man". In other words, character is our deepest existence, which can be transformed, but not deleted. Character has life within itself. It's extremely important that we know that every minute of our existence it remains within us, as well as the different stages of our growth.

Character doesn't decompose, doesn't disappear; it's eternal. Our body decomposes, we can practice our personality, we can mold the temperaments, but not our character, because it is a result, not a method; it is the essence of your being, and it lives forever. Character is all that we are and what we have lived through, and our growth depends on the good formation we may receive.

Character is all that we are and what we have lived through.

Destiny

The final outcome for each individual is destiny. Within every man and every woman there is a right character and a wrong character (a good identity and a bad one).

Paul, one of the greatest teachers of the Christian era, said: "You were taught, with regard to your former way of life, to put off your old self, which is being corrupted by its deceitful desires; to be made new in the attitude of your minds; and to put on the new self, created to be like God in true righteousness and holiness." *(Ephesians 4:22-24 NIV)*

We are not talking about personality here, neither are we talking about two different people; rather we are talking about a substitution. This is the reason why I say that men have two identities, one that represent mortal things such as: fear, dread, addictions, sicknesses, despair, doubts, indifference, anguish, loneliness, sorrow, etc.; and the other that carries eternal things such as: love, faith, hope, joy, temperance, forgiveness, honesty, and assurance, etc.

The inner man that we develop the most is the one who is going to have supremacy over the outer man. That is why I think that change in people doesn't depend only on their attitude, as most motivational speakers say, although everything begins there, but rather on the development of one of the two identities. Who decides what to develop? The outer man through his five senses. Men can hear (hearing), eat (taste), see (sight), feel (touch), and smell (smell), but through their five senses they can choose what they will or will not do. I declare that the man who uses his senses to feed the bad man will perish here and in the next life, but the man who feeds the inner man with God's image, has all the power of the Creator.

If you want to grow in the physical and spiritual world, you have to learn to listen to your inner being. This has all the answers to your questions and doubts. "If any of you lacks wisdom, you should ask God, who gives generously to all without finding fault, and it will be given to you." *(James 1:5 NIV)* A lot has been said about the benefits of talking to God and listening to His voice, but very little has been said about how to have access to Him.

The first thing I want to mention is that God lives in us. *(Galatians 2:20)* I must also say that there is a power in us that surpasses all created things, because we are His vessel, one in which He has deposited His creative force. *(1 Corinthians 3:16)* I was never told what this meant. Simply, what it means is that we are the temple of the Being that covers everything and is the Creator of everything. But, what is a temple? It is a sacred dwelling place. If our body is the dwelling place of the Supreme Being, of the one who governs and created everything, then we have unlimited capacity.

If our body is the dwelling place of the Supreme Being, of the one who governs and created everything, then we have unlimited capacity.

The one who is within us is called the "new man", the "inner man", the one whom I simply call: the right man. For many people, the phrase, "God spoke to me" or "God told me", is a shocking expression, but it should not be, because he lives within us. Why do I tell you all this? Because our final destination depends on our inner man, just as our failures and our growth also depend on how much we can listen to him. He doesn't err, doesn't fail, and lacks nothing. He knows everything. The inner man that you develop more will be the one who determines your destiny. The development of your character is only a result of your present actions. Many people are concerned about their destiny and not their present actions. Be concerned about developing an eternal character; that will be your destiny.

An old man was planting a fruit, and when his neighbor saw him, he made fun of him. He told him that he was a fool if he thought he would get to eat the fruit of the tree he was planting, because by the time the tree would bear fruit, the old man wouldn't be alive. Nevertheless, the wise man said to the man who made fun of him: "I have eaten the fruit of many trees I didn't plant. Someone planted them so that someone else could eat their fruit. Likewise, by planting this tree, I am just repaying some of what life has given to me." That is how you build a good destiny, planting what you won't even be able to eat.

Planting is what guarantees that we will have fruits. The law of sowing and reaping says that, whoever plants a seed expects a fruit of the same kind, in the same proportion as he has planted. If you don't plant anything, don't expect anything. The same happens with your character, and the law of sowing and reaping applies: you will only reap what you sow, no more, nothing different.

In conclusion, the result of everything we decide, and what happens to us, becomes impregnated in us as an identity. And, if we know how to handle it and give it the necessary attention, we will be people without limits, like the Creator. I also want you to know that temperament and character shape your destiny, which will depend on how much you have sown in them.

CHAPTER 4

EVERYTHING IS IN THE MIND

The noblest kind of man has a broad mind.
Anonymous

You are what you have in your mind and also what you think most of the time, because everything you want and who you are is in your mind. The mind is made up of three key identities: the conscious mind, the unconscious mind and the subliminal mind.

Let's look at some graphics that show us what we are saying in a way that we can understand better.

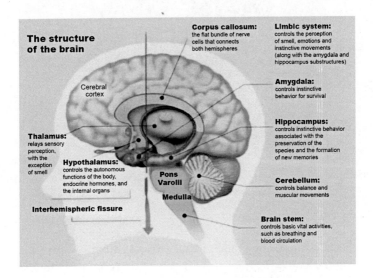

The structure of the brain

Corpus callosum: the flat bundle of nerve cells that connects both hemispheres

Limbic system: controls the perception of smell, emotions and instinctive movements (along with the amygdala and hippocampus substructures)

Cerebral cortex

Amygdala: controls instinctive behavior for survival

Hippocampus: controls instinctive behavior associated with the preservation of the species and the formation of new memories

Thalamus: relays sensory perception, with the exception of smell

Hypothalamus: controls the autonomous functions of the body, endocrine hormones, and the internal organs

Pons Varolii

Medulla

Cerebellum: controls balance and muscular movements

Interhemispheric fissure

Brain stem: controls basic vital activities, such as breathing and blood circulation

When I speak of the mind, I am guided by what many psychologists have called the conscious identity of the brain. According to them, it is what makes the difference between man and other living things.

The conscious mind has to do with our five senses and is subject to the will of man. The unconscious mind has a closer relationship with the subliminal mind, because it has to do with what we don't consciously perceive, but is brought to our mind through the senses.

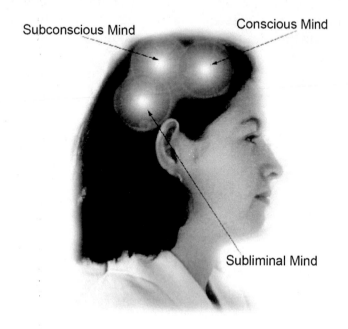

Subconscious Mind

Conscious Mind

Subliminal Mind

Now, we will not define that process for two reasons: first, I am not an expert in psychology or psychiatry; second, I don't intend to give you a class on psychology, anatomy or any similar topic. My intention in this chapter is that we be able to see the potential with which we were born and that we take care of it, paying attention to what we process in our minds. Why? Because the purpose of this book is to achieve more than just a dream, that we don't just remain in theories, but that we know also the formation of each one of our identities, and the process that will help us overcome our fears and limitations.

The conscious mind constitutes 10% of our mind; it only has to do with our senses, with which we decide what we will or will not do. The subconscious mind operates in most of our mind because it retains all the information that is transmitted from our conscious mind and all that is absorbed by our subliminal mind. The subconscious mind is where all our habits are, which is why most of the time we do things unconsciously, guided by our subconscious mind.

I heard a radio program where there was interaction with the audience. A man called and told his story, which, although it was a little sad, was also a little humorous. The man lived with this wife and children on the sixth floor of one of the buildings in Upper Manhattan, in New York City. On the second floor of the same building lived a woman whom this man began to find physically interesting. One day he decided to win her love and the women reciprocated, accepting a date in her own apartment.

The man, seeing that his date was getting close, started commenting in his house that he was going to get another job and that that Friday he had an interview with his new boss. So when Friday came, the man got up at five in the morning, got dressed up, put on cologne, etc. When his wife saw so much grooming, she commented:

"My love, it seems like instead of having a job interview, you are going to have a romantic date."

To which he replied:

"Silly, you are always saying silly things. I have to

look presentable so they give me a good job. Haven't you heard that "clothes make the man"?

"I was only kidding, my love. It seems I cannot even make a joke," said the woman.

The man smiled and kissed her and the children, who were still asleep, and left.

What the wife didn't imagine, however, is that he did have a date with the neighbor who lived in the second floor. So the man went down to the second floor and knocked at the door. The woman opened the door, in this way starting the love affair.

Hours went by and the man was enjoying the intimacy with his new lover. He slept for a while in the bed, then he got up and ate something that the woman had prepared; and all of a sudden, the Casanova forgot that he was on the second floor — of the building where his family lived — with a woman that was not his. In a moment of relaxation when he was resting, wearing a nightgown, the women with whom he was spending the whole day, took a garbage bag and was about to take it out to the patio.

"Where are you going?" He asked.

"To take out the garbage," the woman answered with a smile.

"Oh no, that is a man's job. Give me that garbage," answered the romantic Casanova with a smile.

"Are you sure, my love?" she asked, "You don't need to bother, I do it everyday.

The Casanova answered:

"But I am a gentleman and for that God put me in your path, so you don't trouble yourself anymore.

So the woman gave the garbage bag to the man, and he went down the stairs, so calm, put it in the dumpster and went back to his hiding place. When he got back, he was surprised that the door was closed and locked. So he knocked and waited for his lover to open the door, but to his surprise, it was his wife who was there, who was also surprised to see him. At that moment, he tried to organize his thoughts, he looked everywhere, trying to find an explanation, but at that instant a slap from his wife took him out of his confusion.

"So you are working, huh?" the woman said.

The man did not respond, because his head was still spinning due to his surprise and the slap. On top of that, the door slammed in his face; and it was then that he started to understand what was happening, because the number on that door was not a second-floor number. Without realizing it, he had knocked on the door of his apartment on the sixth floor; and the worst of it was that he was wearing nothing but a nightgown.

The story ends with the man having neither a wife nor a lover. The first one left him, for cheating; the second one left him as well, to avoid problems with the neighbor.

What had happened to this man? His unconscious mind betrayed him. For him, it was a habit to take the garbage out of his apartment wearing his bathrobe. So that day, when he went down, his subconscious mind guided him back home, which was his habit every time he took the garbage out to the dumpster.

The result was that this man, instead of going to the apartment on the second floor, knocked on the door of his apartment on the sixth floor. So he lost his wife and all that he had accomplished with his family up to that day. At the moment he called the radio station, he sounded very discouraged; he was living alone in a rented room, without family. The subconscious mind can make you do things that you would never do consciously.

The same thing happens in regard to our dreams, but in another proportion; people want to accomplish much, but they don't do anything, because they have not been trained for abundance. The subconscious mind is going to give you what has been given to it. No more, no less. If you have lived with hollow dreams, lying about everything in order to get things, trying to get everything the easy way, the unconscious mind will store all that and will give it back to you as soon as possible. You cannot be a successful person unless you have a successful subconscious. To do otherwise is like swimming against the current.

That's why it's important to know that in the subconscious mind there is power like that of ten people like ourselves. So then, if you use the power of your mind in the right way, you have ten new possibilities of achieving anything, even what seems impossible. Now, with this information, you know that you are ten times more powerful than a moment ago. Many are those who want to grow and go far, but they don't know why they don't do it; here is the answer: they have their subconscious mind filled with destructive things and they haven't focused it on the positive. If you focus on the positive, I assure you that you will achieve anything you want.

The mind produces things

The mind produces things that, through the right process, will be seen in the future. What am I saying? That nothing will happen outside you if it doesn't happen first inside you. You are a reflection of what you believe. And, about your beliefs, I have to tell you that in order to be transformed, you need to change your beliefs and let the new information transform your mind. Because remember, you are what you have put in your mind up to now. You can change what you are by changing the information in your mind.

It is very difficult for a person to accept change and admit that he needs it. People fear change so much that when someone mentions something about it, instantly they consider that odd, even when in most cases that person has paid a high price.

If you think that you have done it all, that you don't need anything, that you are a happy woman or a happy man, then this book is not for you; but if you feel that you want to evolve, move forward, grow, then this information is for you. If you want a change and you decide to do it, I assure you that tomorrow you will be a different person. Your future doesn't exist, what really exists is your present.

One day I received a telephone call from a lady. She called because she wanted to ask me if I was going to be in a conference with a motivator. My answer was "yes," we were going to be giving those talks with the hope of helping people to transform their way of thinking to a more positive, happier way of thinking.

The lady didn't tell me anything directly, but indirectly she informed me of many things. She told me that people who go to those conferences are usually depressed people; they are people with a weak mind, losers, etc. So I asked her:

> "Have you had any bad experience with one of those people?"

> "No," she replied.

> "And with the motivator?" I asked her again.

> "No, not with her either," she reiterated.

And then, I said:

> "A few days ago I saw your daughter in one of those lectures and I noticed that she was very motivated. She even told me she wants to motivate others.

> "But my daughter does that because she has a weak mind and she lives depressed," she said.

I realized that I wasn't going to get anywhere trying to reason with her. She wouldn't understand no matter how much I tried to explain, because if the change she saw in her daughter didn't help, what else could have helped?

"Be transformed by the renewing of your mind." *(Romans 12:2 WEB)* For a person to be changed, he needs to make a decision to transform his mind. While I was listening to a motivational CD, I heard a phrase that really captivated me: "Think, talk and act like the person you want to be until you become that person." *(Alex Day)*

Everything that comes to our lives is profoundly related to how we think and who we are. Your mind produces what you want it to produce; no one can change that, not even God himself. You are master of yourself and you have the ability to think, believe, and act as you please. I have had somewhat unpleasant experiences with many parents; they have asked me: "Please counsel my son because he has a lot of problems." But when I make an appointment and go to their house, I come across the phenomenon that they don't even want to listen to me; in fact, many of them stay in their rooms and never come out.

When a person doesn't want to change, no one can do it for them. The parents, even with all their love, make a big mistake with their children; they want to change them, but they don't understand that only their children can decide to do that. No one can produce in you something that they haven't put in your mind, and if they don't give it the freedom to process itself.

Our mind makes us unique

In our mind we have emotions, understanding, thoughts, reasoning, perception, memory, imagination, will, and other cognitive skills. We already talked about the subconscious mind, what the Bible calls the "old man" *(Ephesians 4:22–24)* who, according to this writer, is corrupted. What does that mean? If the subconscious mind is a storehouse, that means that everything that the conscious mind lets in, gets stored in it. It becomes the engine of human behavior; which means the senses become the canals through which it is fed.

When a child is born, it isn't born with an empty mind as many people claim, because — whether for good or for bad — children come with patterns that they got from the mother in the womb. Christians call this "original sin." Those tendencies develop as the child grows, strengthening in the subconscious mind and forming powerful habits. The behavior patterns of a child are very weak, which is why they can be fought against easily. That's why it is easier for a child to change than for an adult.

For instance, a child believes, loves, forgives, helps, smiles, and changes from one state of mind to another with ease. A child can be crying and, a moment later, when the parents give him a candy or a toy, without thinking, he can wipe his tears and smile. A child is capable of believing anything.

The behavior patterns of a child are very weak, which is why they can be fought against easily. That is why it is easier for a child to change than for an adult.

Suppose a father, for instance, stands in front of his child and tells him: "I've been taking a class to learn to jump from a ten-story building, and I have learned that nothing will happen to me if I did it. The only thing I have to do is wear the Superman cape and I will be ready to go. What if I buy one for me and one for you?" Then the father buys two capes and tells the child: "Wear one, I will wear the other, and get on my back so we can start flying."

I assure you that if that child has had a good relationship with his father, he will do it. That is the ability to believe that children have. Regardless of what you do to him, or the pain you have caused, everything will fade away when he feels your arms around his body. Jesus, the Master, said: "Assuredly, I say to you, unless you are converted and become as little children, you will by no means enter the Kingdom of heaven." *(Matthew 18:3 NKJV)* Therefore, whoever lacks the ability to believe like a child, will not enter the kingdom of God.

We have said that the "old man" (the unconscious mind) is corrupted. Why? Because it has been fed with trauma, pain, resentment, remorse: things we have stored in our brain and that prevent us from progressing to the level we have set for ourselves. "For what I will to do, that I do not practice; but what I hate, that I do." *(Romans 7:15 NKJV)* Most people are controlled by habits; the problem is that bad habits operate in the subconscious mind. The wrong information, patterns and habits that are in your mind are the obstacles that keep you from reaching your goals.

How to heal the subconscious mind

The subconscious mind is fed with everything you have heard, seen, touched, tasted, smelled. In your short or long life, you are what you have put in it. Every man and woman is the product of what he or she has acquired through knowledge. All those bad habits that are acquired from our mother's womb are what the Bible calls the "old man," or the "man of sin," that subjugate the natural man to his natural mind.

However, we have the possibility of renewing our minds, of cultivating new habits, of assembling the "new man created to be like God." If all the bad comes as a set of wrong beliefs, the good will also come from right beliefs. The new man, the inner child, is fed with right knowledge, which will be manifested in right attitudes, because all the knowledge that is processed in your being is going to be manifested as a creative or destructive action.

All the attributes or fruits of the Eternal One are powerful forces that will enable man to be healed of any disease, plus they give him that prosperous, full and happy life that he is searching for so much.

Does it happen or do we think it does?

Events are part of our lives and we can't stop them. Every day, good things and bad things happen around us and we can't control that. But we can control the things that happen inside us. Although you can't avoid the negative things that happen in this world, you can avoid the negative things that happen in your world.

Although you can't avoid the negative things that happen in this world, you can avoid the negative things that happen in your world.

When I talk in front of an audience, I always think about the fact that it is a diverse audience, because while I speak, I notice that all of them see and feel something different. The event is one, the speaker is one, but the interpretations are many, and that is due to the fact that "every mind is a world unto itself."

Each time I speak, I see people who are motivated; others go out wiping away their tears, some criticizing, but there is always one whose face looks as if one of his family members had been killed. There is always someone who is offended by some or all of what I said; someone who thinks that my only goal was to make him feel bad. What impresses me is not the people and their reactions, but the fact that at one single event there have been so many reactions.

This makes it clear that when we speak about success or growth, or when we want a person to be educated in the teachings of a religion, a business or a discipline, it is important to take into consideration that not all think alike and that every person has different perceptions, as well. The events that are happening are not what makes us feel good or bad, successful or unsuccessful, but what we are really interpreting is what will take us to a better future, whatever may be the life we have chosen to live. What you see is your reality.

A clear example of that is when I talk to someone who doesn't see things the way I do. The first thing I have put in my mind is that that person is not bad, or dumb, but that he or she is seeing everything in a different way. The interpretation of things is more important than the things themselves. Nothing that happens around us can hurt us; what we do with what happens to us is what can destroy us. When we focus on a problem, we move away from the solution. Understanding that we will always be okay, and that God put the Universe at our service, is an important step.

To maintain a positive attitude toward life is to have faith. "Now, faith is confidence in what we hope for and assurance about what we do not see." *(Hebrews 11:1 NIV)* Thus, we must always expect the best of life, expect that everything is and will be okay, and that we will always achieve our goals. The events of this world may not offer the best outlook; the economy, politics, social and immigration problems — among others — make you feel as if you are going to collapse, but if you keep believing and persevering, you will make it, because he who perseveres, succeeds. He who perseveres until the end will have it all.

In conclusion, your mind can help you to obtain good or evil; it can help you to live healthy or sick, sad or happy, lonely or accompanied, rich or poor. Your mind can become your friend or your enemy. Your mind is used for believing or for fearing. Your mind creates things, that is why you must learn to create the best; anyway, if God gave you a mind, it is so you will use it in the right way.

CHAPTER 5

I THINK, I TALK AND I ACT

The human body is the carriage, the real me, the man who drives it; the thoughts are the reins, and the feelings are the horses.

Plato

The words in the title are in the correct order; things can't go through your mouth before going through your mind as a thought. The mouth just executes what your brain has processed. "For out of the abundance of the heart, the mouth speaks." *(Matthew 12:34 ESV)* Ideas go through your mind first and then they take form in your mouth; the mouth is what gives form to the thoughts. In order to achieve what we want, it is very important to take action, because "faith without works is dead." *(James 2:26 NASB)*

I met a very intelligent man with many good ideas. He would convince anyone just by talking, but he was full of fear. He would not put his ideas into action, and he died without seeing his plans accomplished. God has never promised to bless thoughts or plans, but He promises to bless the actions you take, the fruit of your hands. Every action brings a reaction. In other words, a good action brings good results; a bad action, bad results; no action, no results.

Our life is the result of our actions. Believe it or not, every time a thought comes to our mind, it will want to produce a result; therefore, we are the ones who need to evaluate our thoughts to obtain good results.

"I think, I talk and I act," is a formula that allows us to know the correct order to achieve things. If you analyze your thoughts well, good words will come out and the result will be good actions. Don't allow negative thoughts to take control of you. Let them fly around your head, but don't let them make a nest in your hair. Thoughts will always come to our minds, but we are the ones responsible for allowing the thoughts we want to stay.

We have to use our senses to control our thoughts. Someone told me once, that he was able to stop his thoughts completely and leave his mind empty, but that isn't possible. What is possible is to put our thoughts on a slower pace, but not stop them, because the human mind is never empty, since it never stops working.

The guarantee of success

While I was giving a series of lectures in Cienfuegos, a sector of Santiago, in the Dominican Republic, a man who smelled very much of alcohol said he wanted to talk to me. When I finished greeting the people who were around me, I approached the man, who was still waiting for me with great anxiety reflected on his face. Immediately he told me:

> "Today I went out of the house to get drunk, to go back home and kill my wife and children."

"Why?" I said.

> "Because my wife cheated on me with another man, and I can't stand it, that's why I want to kill her. But while I was walking by, I saw that this place was open, I noticed that there were people and I thought that something good could happen to me here. That is why I came in, and while I was listening, I changed my mind and I don't want to do anything wrong anymore.

"Are you sure you no longer want to kill her?" I insisted.

I asked that question to make sure he would not try anything bad, because if I had seen any indication of danger to that family, I would have reported him immediately.

> "Don't you believe what you teach?" he said. You yourself said that there is hope for every man who can believe. You said that it is never too late to change, that today is the best day to have an opportunity and start dreaming of a better future.

The man asked me to visit his wife, and, since I was going to be in the community the whole week, I assured him that I would do so.

The next day I visited the woman and talked to her about the change her husband had professed that he would make, but the woman did not believe me at all; she was incredulous. She could not believe that a man with a life like her husband's could change, because he was a rough and tough man without much affection.

When I saw her like that, I told her: "You have to believe, because the one who believes can move mountains of difficulties." And it's true; there is an unequalled power in the person who believes. A mind that believes is capable of creating things. There are people who get alarmed when I say this, but what I want them to understand is that concepts only take shape in our mind. Without the mind, believing is not possible; that's one of the reasons why everything that happens under the sun is caused by a person. We are the only living beings who have a mind, and only what our mind is capable of believing is likely to occur.

Nothing happens unless you believe it. Everything that happens is because it was already conceived in our mind. The wife of Mr. José decided to go to the conferences and, after five days, her home and all their lives were different; they had changed. What happened in this home? They heard that there was a possibility of change and they decided to believe it. Life only gives us what we believe can happen. Believing that something can happen is what finally makes things happen. Don't start doing something if you don't believe it can happen.

There are people who have grudges, hatred, pain, traumas, etc., deeply rooted in the subconscious mind, but they ignore that they have them, even though they feel them. Of course, that makes them live a tormented life. When we don't take all these evils out of our mind and we allow them to have a nest there, we prevent the growth that we could be experiencing daily. But, how do we do the opposite? How do we get rid of those barriers and improve? It is very simple. We should properly feed our inner child, talk to it, make it feel loved and cherished; allow it to grow in wisdom, peace, goodness and faith, and surely it will be able to change our whole being.

Many people think that they can feed the inner child only with prayer and study. However, that implies a serious problem. The problem is that if we don't give it the right food, the result or growth will not be right, either. Prayer is a very useful tool in any religion, as well as study. I, as a Christian, consider the study of the Bible to be a vital tool for the strengthening of one's soul, one's intentions and most of all, one's intellect. I have seen people who have been greatly educated through it.

But this tool must be used properly, otherwise entirely the opposite of what we desire will occur.

I consider the study of the Bible to be a vital tool for the strengthening of one's soul, one's intentions, and most of all, one's intellect.

An example of what I am trying to say is the case of some people who have lost their memory by studying certain passages and texts. These are so profound, and the people who try to study them don't have the proper training to understand, and therefore, they can't analyze them without God's help. There are also people who use prayers in an incorrect way, since they spend most of their time telling God to solve their problems, and they don't cease to mention one problem after another.

This is not good because you are strengthening the one who focuses on himself like this. If you think too much about something or someone, what you are doing is strengthening that thing or person. That is why so many people — though they are men and women who call themselves believers — all they do is see and receive negative things in their lives, because they only think about negative things. Therefore, whatever you do, do it through an outlook of positive faith.

Now, let it not be a faith in what your physical eyes are seeing, but in what you know you can be or can become. By the way, I clarify the topic about positive faith, because there is a negative faith which we can call fear. That negative faith has the same power as positive faith, but in a destructive way.

When you go to God in prayer, don't present yourself with the same list of requests for the things you need; ask only one time, and then give thanks for what you are expecting. Declare it affirmatively as if you already had it. Instead of saying, "Give me a car," say: "Thanks for the car that is on its way." Oh, and don't forget to think about details such as model, year, color, etc. Be specific and you will get it that way. Remember that if you don't know what you want, it will not come to you. Would you settle for anything? That's why the details of what you ask for are important at the moment that you request it.

I suggest that you always use these three powers that the Eternal One has given you. The first one is the power of gratitude; thank God for all the things that happen to you and all the things you have. The second power you have to use on this earth is the power of receiving. "Ye ask, and receive not, because ye ask amiss." *(James 4:3 KJV)* Many people don't receive what they ask for because, A) they are only trying to satisfy their selfish heart. I want to clarify that I am not talking about things that were made for us to enjoy, but I am talking about those who want more in order to humiliate others and feel superior to them. B) They don't receive because they don't feel worthy of having anything. Although it seems incredible, it is true: having a disposition to receive and always expecting the best, will make it happen. The third power is the power of believing. Only those who believe they can achieve things will do so.

If your prayers are focused on these three powers, you will have anything you ask for and you will heal any illness. When you give thanks even for people who have hurt you, and choose an attitude of forgiveness and selflessness in your heart, everything will change and your heart will be at peace.

What you think about yourself tells what you are going to receive

While pastoring a church, I was invited to attend a study group that several people were having on Saturday evenings. I arrived at the place; an older woman was going to give the talk that evening. Her exposition was entitled, "We are like a worm," and the Scripture she quoted was a portion of the Bible taken from the Book of Job. While I observed the response of the people who were there, it seemed to me that they were very happy with such a great discovery.

The lady, being aware that I had graduated from a university with a degree in Theology, and wanting to increase the credibility she was already having with the people, deferentially asked my opinion about what she was teaching and, since I didn't like the way she had discussed the subject, I told her it was okay; but, it seemed to me everyone had understood, therefore explanations were unnecessary. (In reality, I didn't want to hurt that lady, because my opinion was very different from hers.) The lady insisted, and even told me that she was not going to get offended if my opinion was different from hers.

Then I said:

> "Dear friend, I want you to know that God doesn't want His children to believe what you have said."

"But ... it is in the Bible," she replied.

"No, not everything that is in the Bible comes from God," I said.

The woman put her hand on her mouth, shocked, looking at me as the worst of blasphemers:

"How is that?" she said, by now irritated.

"One example of that is the text you just read," I said; "the one who talks is Job, not God. The patriarch, amid numerous negative experiences, feels depressed and talks disparagingly about himself."

In the Bible there are several cases of people who got depressed and thought that they were nothing and nobody. For instance, we have Elijah in the cave, Jeremiah in his lamentations; Isaiah with his vision of exile, etc. God only takes responsibility for whatever is good, whatever is just, whatever is lovely, whatever is admirable. If you want to grow the new man that is in you, the one who dreams, the one who grows, the one who progresses, the one who wants to be happy, the one who wants a good marriage, you have to think about whatever is pure, whatever is lovely, whatever is of a good report. Just think about that, not about the rest.

We can be believers and practicants of any religion, but if we are unhappy, the rest is useless. Happiness is something we cannot afford to lose. Happiness is the state of mind most sought after. Therefore, what's the use of having everything if you are not happy? We have to strike a balance between what we want and the way to get there.

God is inside you, and that means you are a special being created like Him, after His image and likeness. So, if that is the case, then you already are a happy person. However, if you are not happy, that means that the child inside you has not been fed in accordance with God. That food is His word. "For the word of God is quick and powerful and sharper than any twoedged sword, piercing even to the dividing asunder of soul and spirit, and of the joints and marrow, and is a discerner of the thoughts and intents of the heart." *(Hebrews 4:12 KJV)*

Now, when those intentions are well-guided, we can change all the complexes, frustrations, depressions, and heal any disease — not only in our body, but also in our mind — and overcome all the obstacles that we face in life. God represents whatever is good; therefore, any person who does something good, does it because He has spoken to him. When a person doesn't focus on the good, he is missing out on the power that the Creator has given him as his inheritance.

Do not forget that, if you focus on negative things, on the problems or on your faults, you will be strengthening those evils. What you focus on is what you strengthen. Every word you speak, every thing you see, if it's focused on your defects, you will be strengthening those evils. What you focus on is what you strengthen — a part of you that can be either positive or negative, a good or a bad man, a strong or a weak man, a successful or unsuccessful man. You must decide today, you cannot postpone it for another day; you must decide at this moment what you are going to do with the rest of your life.

If you focus on negative things, on the problems or on your faults, you will be strengthening those evils. What you focus on is what you strengthen.

Inside you, you have everything you need to succeed. You have all the resources inside you, not outside. That is why I always say that there are no poor countries; there are poor people, because even the most devastated countries, at one time had all the resources they needed to become prosperous. The inner man has to be fed, not repressed or punished, because he is not your enemy; he is your friend. He is waiting for you in order to give you his help. "Righteousness and love have kissed each other," *(see Psalms 85:10)* therefore, there should be no conflict between you and him; that must disappear.

That, however, is true at some stage in our life; for instance, when we were like fickle children, who fought; *(Romans 7:14)* but now we have peace, because we made the decision to strengthen the new man and weaken the old man, the one who brought our failures, frustrations, pains, sicknesses, fears, and all those things we drag around with us and that paralyze our growth and success. When you think, talk, and act based on something, you are putting all your efforts into that, and for sure, you will achieve it because that is the correct process.

CHAPTER 6

SUCCESS IS WITHIN YOU

I've failed over and over and over again in my life, and that is why I succeed.
Michael Jordan

In order to receive success inside us and then see it outside (since everything is born within us first), the first thing we have to do is believe that inside us there are qualities of greatness, given that man is like his Creator. In the story of creation, which is found in the first chapters of the Bible, it says that man was made in the image and likeness of the One who created him.

One thing that's very true is that you are what you are made of. And if you don't know what that is, I want to tell you what we are made of. According to the Genesis account, the Creator took clay and made a doll and breathed his breath into its nostrils, and the doll was given life. That doll became a being in the image and likeness of the Being who created him. *(Genesis 2:7)* But, what is this man made of? He is made of divine matter and substance. So the clay is the image and the substance is the likeness.

The physical says a lot about where we want to go; we already talked about that when we talked about personality, but I would like to add that if you are the kind of person who eats whatever, someone who doesn't take care of his body by eating good food, who doesn't exercise regularly; if you have neglected your personal appearance, that may affect your future negatively. In fact, those deficiencies limit your ability to have the success you want to have. Understanding the fact that because we have divine substance, our body not only depends on the physical, but it also has regenerative power; and if we know how to focus and release it by faith, we may be surprised by the results.

One example of what I am saying is that some people

start by pretending and they end up believing their own lies. I have seen people who begin pretending they have a problem in one of their legs, and they end up having pain precisely in that leg; they start with a cane and end up crippled.

When I came to the United States, I noticed that a countless number of people used canes; when I continued analyzing the phenomenon, I realized that — although not in all cases — that happens because in this country the government gives financial aid to people with disabilities. Now, the mere fact of knowing that every month they are going to get money for walking with a cane, causes the people not to be healed, nor do they even strive to achieve it. (Once again, I want to clarify: I am not generalizing or judging those who really are sick).

When I broaden my focus a little and compare this situation with that of my country, I realize that in the Dominican Republic the number of people with disabilities is minimal. The reason is that because in my country no one gets paid for being sick. Now, the question we must ask ourselves is: what would happen if we were to use that power in business, with our beliefs or when we want to achieve a goal? We would have a life of successes with unlimited resources.

People achieve what they want in life, even in spite of having a disability or a disease. Self-reliance has an infinite power for good or for evil. It is important to know this, because you feed what you want to achieve or what you want to live. Every time you get up in the morning, make statements that strengthen how you want to live the rest of your day. We can affirm that this is a self-fulfilling prophecy.

People achieve what they want in life, even in spite of having a disability or a disease.

Life is simple: make a decision and don't go back. The indecisive and confused person who doesn't know what he really wants, in the end, gets that: indecision, confusion, etc., because he who doesn't know what he wants is already there; just like the one who doesn't know where he is coming from, doesn't know where he is going.

You are who you think you are

Once, a mother of a young lady asked me to visit her daughter because her boyfriend had dumped her and she had fallen into a deep depression. The girl wouldn't come out of her room; she barely ate, and would only speak to very few people. The young lady had put in her mind the idea that she was ugly and that no one loved her.

Politely I accepted the lady's invitation, and when we arrived at her house (I want to clarify that this family was in a very comfortable economic position), the mother grabbed my hand and took me to the room where the girl was. We got to the center of the room, where the bed was; she sat down by her precious daughter, and she made a gesture for me to get closer to where she was. She made me sit on the bed, beside the girl, who was wrapped in the sheets with her face covered.

When I sat down, immediately the mother got up and told me: "Here is my daughter, please help her." And she left the room in a hurry. I tried to stop her, but it was too late. The lady had left the room, which is why I stayed alone in a room with a woman I didn't know, whom I had never seen before, and who only talked and thought about suicide because nobody loved her.

A little scared, and with a look of terror I just couldn't shake off, a comforting idea came to my head: "If this girl is depressed because her boyfriend left her for being ugly, it must be because she really is ugly." So, leaving behind my fears, I started talking to her:

"Did you know that you are an extraordinary person? That you are not valuable for what you have, but for who you are? That what people think about you is not what makes you who you are, that that is not what gives value to your life? You are who you are because your Creator made you that way, from a unique mold, with an exclusive destiny, a purpose of your own and an exceptional life that you can enjoy and be happy."

You are who you are because your Creator made you that way, from a unique mold, with an exclusive destiny, a purpose of your own and an exceptional life that you can enjoy and be happy.

I paused to see her reaction, and that was when I had the biggest surprise of my life. The girl started taking her head out of the sheets while I was getting ready to see the next actress for the horror movies. But, when she finally took her face out of that hiding place, she was the one who was horrified. That's because the cry I let out shook her. I said, "Mamma mia!" But it was not because I was scared, but because I was surprised to see such a beautiful young lady.

As we struck up a conversation, and when she pulled the sheet aside, I saw that she had a pretty figure, a pretty face, and a youthfulness in the prime of life. She was so beautiful that she could star in any role on film or television. However, she had a wrong attitude about the true value of human beings.

She saw herself as ugly, and that is what she was. You are who you believe you are, and you are what are you made of. These two ideas show us the relationship that exists between the mind and the body, between your emotions and your physiognomy. Later I will inform you how to take advantage of this; how the spiritual gives life to matter, and why it is that, through this, the spiritual is manifested in the physical world. What am I saying? That visualization and faith, which are two spiritual entities, exist only in another dimension, where they cannot be reached by the physical eye. That is the reason why people who achieve great things aren't understood by most people. They see in themselves and others, attributes, riches and resources that no one else sees.

Wealth and greatness are only for those who can see them

There is a physical reality and a spiritual one; physical reality reaches the third dimension, but the spiritual one is in the fourth dimension and this can only be accessed thought faith and visualization.

In order to be able to find that dimension, one has to believe that there is a spiritual world that transcends the physical world. One example of this is the phenomena which many of us know of as the appearances of angels, healings, deliverances and miraculous phenomena that happen to many people on the physical plane. There are many stories like this in the Bible. In the book of Daniel, chapter 9, it talks about this; also, John says that Jesus came into where the disciples were without being seen, even though they were in a place where the door was locked. *(John 20:19)*

Hagar, Abraham's servant with whom he had had a child, while she was travelling in the desert — when it seem like her child was going to die of thirst — looked steadily at an angel who appeared to her and told her to lift up her eyes. The story says that when she obeyed, her eyes were opened and she saw a well of water from which she and her son drank. *(Genesis 21:19)* Jacob, for instance, saw a stairway, with its top reaching to heaven and the angels of God ascending and descending on it. *(Genesis 28:12)* Also King Belshazzar saw the fingers of a human hand that wrote a message on the plaster of the wall. *(Daniel 5:5)* What I'm saying with all these examples is that, there is a world in another dimension that you and I can't see with our natural eyes, a dimension that a man can't explain, but to which he can have access through visions and faith.

When I was very little, every time something caught my attention, I asked how it was created. I wanted to know the creative process of everything I saw. My grandmother always told me that God had created everything. I kept asking. She kept telling me: "God created that, and everything, from nothing." That answer was too confusing for me. But the funny thing is that because I would keep asking, "What is nothing?" my grandmother always answered the same thing: "Nothing is nothing."

Yet, the interesting thing is that the Bible says the same thing as my grandmother, although in a different way. The Bible said it long before my grandmother, of course. The Scripture declares that God made everything out of what cannot be seen. *(Hebrews 11:3 CEV)* The "nothing" that my grandmother talked about, is actually what God talks about as "what cannot be seen". That is, there is a world behind your world; that world is real, but not everyone can see it. In that world there is no lack of any kind, no diseases, nor pain, nor poverty, nor failures, etc. And you can have access to that world only by faith.

The "nothing" that my grandmother talked about, is actually what God talks about as "what cannot be seen". That is, there is a world behind your world; that world is real, but not everyone can see it.

All the money you need, the house, the car, the vacations, are available for you; you only have to learn to attract the things that are unseen and call those that don't exist as if they existed — those that are hidden from your physical eyes. Let's look at an example. When I get to a place with my wife and children and there is no parking available, I always say out loud: "Even before we were born, God had already reserved a parking spot for us on this day and in this place," And that parking place appears. When I forget to say this phrase, my wife says it. And I know that tomorrow our children will say the same thing.

The same applies for all our needs. All of them were met already, from long before we were born. In the book of Hebrews it says that the men walked in the desert with many needs, but they were happy. They suffered thirst, hunger, and were in danger from serpents, scorpions, lions and plagues, because they could see and greet a better country. *(Hebrews 11)* Those men were happy, not because of what they had at that moment, but for what they knew they would have. That's the key for a dreamer and a successful man: he lives in the present as happy as if he had already achieved his dreams, because he has already been in the place of his dreams.

The story goes that in the opening ceremony of a new attraction at one of the Disney parks, the engineer in charge of the celebration said: "How would Walt Disney feel if he had seen this?" The widow of the entertainment genius, who was by the engineers' side, corrected him by saying: "No, engineer, make no mistake; Walt saw this long before you did."

More than just words

For many people words are nothing more than innumerable sounds that are produced in the vocal cords. However, they are more than that. They are the power of the Creator in our mouth. Words reflect who we are and what we achieve because they come from the depths of our being and they are the embodiment of our thoughts. God is spirit and He lives in the spiritual side of men, not in the natural. Man is like the One who created him and that makes him a being with unlimited powers. That is why every time I feel sad, almost useless, or when fear invades me or I want to feel depressed, I search in my being for who I am. And, what am I? Joy, peace, patience, love, kindness, goodness, gentleness, temperance, confidence, light, optimism, enthusiasm, freedom, health, beauty, etc.

When we were talking about the unconscious mind, I stated that in it there are hidden all the destructive concepts that we have inherited, spoken, acquired, learned and practiced during our entire life. All those concepts come alive when they become habits that shape human character. Likewise, words that are positive, good and pure take shape in the unconscious mind, establishing knowledge, habits, and good and positive attitudes.

Words come out of our hearts, where we also have bad tendencies such as lust, enmities, disputes, anger, conflicts, strife, fears, hatred, low self-esteem, feelings of guilt, grudges, adultery, fornication and uncleanness. All those evils can be changed by the power of God, the same power we have in our words.

When people seek God and don't get results, it is because they have forgotten that God already lives within us, and that we only have to accept Him and put Him into practice through what He has given us, His Spirit, which is nurtured with the word. The word is a great tool; which is why we should not take it lightly. I want to make clear that I believe that the universe is His creation and that all his control is not limited to our inner being. However, I believe that His purposes with us go first. Nevertheless, if we don't understand the power that is within us, we will not fulfill His purpose, either, even though He has all the power in the world.

Many people think that they can do things outside themselves with words, but words can only affect the exterior world after they have been planted in the interior. When I titled this chapter with the phrase, "Success is within you", I did it because I was thinking about this: that everything mentioned in this chapter is expressed in words, nonetheless, they are more than words. For instance, love is expressed with one word, but it can transform a human being, a life. Love is the force that sustains everything, and makes things subsist. You can't achieve anything unless you love it first. So, a person who can't conceive love can hardly utter the word, and if he does utter it, it will not have the necessary power to confirm it.

The power is in the word, as long as one of the forces that move the world for good or for evil can accompany it. Good words create good things. Bad words create bad things. Positive words create positive things. Negative words create evil things. This is a universal law, and if somebody wants to change it, he will have to become God and have his own planet. However, if you want everything to go well in life, follow this law, the law of words, the law that says: you will always have and be whatever comes out of your mouth; because as the thoughts and words of a man are, so is he.

We conclude by saying that the power is within you, because within every human being reside all the qualities that he needs to overcome the impossible.

Besides, every quality that man has is a strength of the One who created him, who is able to do anything.

CHAPTER 7

MORE THAN A SALESPERSON

To be prepared is half the victory.
Miguel de Cervantes

We live in a world of consumers, where every day we are encouraged to consume more and more. Television, Internet, radio, and other means of mass communication ceaselessly promote the products of large enterprises, whose budgets are extremely high.

That's why in the world where we live people become frantic consumers; that's why in these days many people purchase things without knowing what they are acquiring or why they are buying it. Indirectly, that means that sales are becoming an easier profession, although many people think otherwise. What reasons do I have for saying this? One of the reasons is because the unconscious mind works silently and every time an advertisement comes on — in any means of communication — it is not only producing a desire to acquire that product, but in the long run, it is opening the heart of the consumer to feel sympathy toward shopping.

That's the reason why any salesperson, no matter what he sells or how well prepared he is, he will sell to 10% of the people he visits. That's what makes sales a profession for everyone. This law conforms to the law of averages: of every ten people to whom you talk to make a proposal, one will be interested in it. So then, the only thing a person needs to advance in life is to be ambitious and to be able to talk to as many people as possible.

We all sell something

I have always listened to people who have a phobia of sales. The first reason is because they think of sales as an exchange of an item for money. The second reason is because they think of sales as something that will tarnish their reputation. They have had bad experiences with salesmen or companies that have sold them some item.

A friend of mine whose job was selling books, every time he went to a house and was asked if he was a salesman, would answer that he was not. Immediately he would say to the person who had asked him, that he was bringing education and health. Although he had good results in his sales and his words would convince the client, he would not stop the client from thinking what they already thought about a salesman: that he is a thief, a liar, disloyal, a person who is doing that work because he has no education and no other possibilities to find another job. However, the truth is that — whether we accept it or not — we are all salespeople.

Perhaps you say that you have never been a salesman. Then, let me tell you that you live under a bridge; you have never achieved anything for yourself; you don't have a wife; you don't have a job, etc. Because to accomplish anything in this world, you always have to sell something; your belongings, your image, your car, your house, your books, your computer or your ideas which, in fact, even though many people don't give them much importance, are the most expensive possessions you have, even though most of the time you waste them.

Anyway, we are all salesmen; therefore, we sell something, although it may not be the way we make a living. Why do I say this? The first reason is that if you do sales or any other activity that has to do with growth through business, or if the work you do has to do with talking and convincing people, you should not be ashamed of your profession, because you are doing the only work that is in favor of achieving your dreams, and the only profession that doesn't have unemployment. In all the companies of the world they need salespeople and people who focus others on personal growth and the growth of the company. We are the force that drives them, and without us they would not subsist.

I am proud of my job

When I was an adolescent, I would get up at five in the morning to go to a school that had been opened in my hometown. I would ride about ten kilometers on my bicycle to enter at 7:30 in the morning and leave at 1:00 in the afternoon. Then I would go home to eat, and then back to high school. I had one hour to eat and travel 14 kilometers, then leave school and go to work for six hours in the warehouse of Mr. Manuel Mena, who paid me fifty pesos per week (the equivalent of 40 dollars, because I also worked all day during the weekends). I would travel all those miles on the latest model of nickel-plated bicycle, because at that time that was all I could afford. The effort was so great that that bicycle became my most hated vehicle.

In the school where I was going in the mornings, I was getting technical training in line drawings, cabinetmaking, and finish painting. When I was almost finishing my two years of studies, in the summer vacations of high school, the technical institute staff informed us that we had to finish our studies in a high school located in San Francisco de Macoris, the main northeast city of the Dominican Republic.

Since my mother made me go to church with her on the last day of every week, I explained to the teachers that I wasn't going to be able to attend that day. Nevertheless, in spite this, the teachers told me they would not let me graduate, although they would let me finish my education, because there were only two weeks left; in other words, I didn't have the right to get the diploma for which I had worked so hard (I was always one the top three students). That day I begged the teachers to let me graduate; it was only two days that I wasn't going to attend; but they refused. Also, they and the other students mocked me ruthlessly for accompanying my mother to church. That day I cried nonstop in front of everyone, which aggravated the situation.

In this life there are three types of people who are always going to be close to you:

1. Those who, when you present them with an idea, always tell you that you can't, that you don't have the means, that you aren't competent. They don't believe in your talents, or in your dreams, which, by the way, no one is obligated to believe in. This is the group of the pessimists.

2. Those who tell you that there's not much chance of success, but to go ahead and try, to see what happens. The "let's see" group.

3. The optimistic, who are the ones who believe in you and encourage you to keep on going.

In any case, your success always depends on what you have inside. However, it is good to be surrounded by positive people and those who want the best for us.

Although they told me that I was not going to graduate, I finished the remaining two weeks of studies and forgot about the matter. Two years had passed, but since I didn't have a cabinetmaker or painter diploma, I had to start selling books. Besides, they were giving the opportunity for students who wanted to go to college. The plan was to sell books during the summer months, so that those who reach a goal, had the right to study two semesters at the university. That is how I started this wonderful profession, which God has used to this day to achieve all my goals, and what I have left to accomplish, which is a lot.

It was a sunny afternoon when I was going from Santiago de los Treinta Caballeros (the main city of the north, and second in the Dominican Republic) to my hometown in Cotui in a public transportation vehicle. Two men boarded the vehicle; they were two of my former teachers; and they were sweating. I immediately greeted them and they recognized me immediately.

> "What do you do?" Juan asked me (the names have been changed).

> "I sell books," I answered, "and study Theology at the University."

One of them, Pedro, started laughing uproariously.

> "Do you remember Marcos?" he continued

saying, "he is now working in a very nice shop; while you, for being a 'pariguayo,'[1] are selling books and studying Theology."

The two teachers laughed at me until they couldn't breathe. They didn't think about the fact that there were other people in the vehicle, or how I felt, but I kept quiet without being bothered. Their words were not my motor, I knew what I was doing and what I wanted to accomplish. Besides, although they laughed at my new occupation, I was earning more money working during the summer than the money the two of them were earning in a year.

Two years went by, I got married and stopped living on campus at the university to go back to my hometown, which obligated me to commute 70 miles. Then I bought my second car, a Toyota Camry with tinted windows, embellishments in the windows and very well equipped. In my country, that was a dream that not many people could accomplish, but with my occupation of selling books, as well as the blessing of God, that was possible.

One afternoon of heavy rain, when I was going back from the university, I saw two people getting wet alongside the road while they were trying to get a lift; they were my former teachers. To be honest, I only stopped because I was overcome by my pride. I wanted the people who had humiliated me so much to see my new car and let them know that in spite of their destructive words, their haughtiness, their mocking and lack of consideration, I was able to get ahead, to achieve my goals.

[1] *Pariguayo: Word used in the Dominican Republic to refer to a person who is gullible.*

Besides, I was dying to rub in their faces that I didn't need the diploma that I had worked so hard to get and they had refused to give me, remember? But when they got in the car, something within me changed. Those two men were going home from work, they were soaking wet, and I shouldn't act toward them the same way they did toward me, because the opportunities we take advantage of, and the achievements we attain in life are not to humiliate others, but to inspire them.

Immediately after they got in the car and looked up to see who was the driver, I noticed that they were overwhelmed with surprise and shame; I could see it on their faces. We talked for a long time on the way, and the same professor who had made fun of me, put his hand on my shoulder and told me: "I knew you were the best."

This didn't end there. About two months later, one of them came to my house and told me that that month they were going to hold a graduation ceremony and that I could go to the graduation to receive my diploma. Although I didn't go, nor did I ask for anything, they sent it to my house. Today, however, I have the satisfaction of telling you about this experience. It is probably your experience, too. I know that those who dare to do something in life are always attacked by someone who wants to take away their dreams. And when it comes to sales, many people are ashamed of what they do because they consider their work inferior. Be proud of any work you perform. Work dignifies a man, it doesn't humiliate him.

Be proud of any work you perform. Work dignifies a man, it doesn't humiliate him.

I must tell you, however, that every person who strives in life, and feels proud of his work, will achieve success. In fact, one of the keys of success is to tell everyone about what you are passionate about, because the piece that you need to put your puzzle together might be in front of you.

Against all odds

Everybody prepares to succeed; no one prepares to fail. On the other hand, what gives us success is not the times when things don't go well, but the times when things don't go wrong. Yet, this helps us to learn new ways of doing things, so that we do them better and better. And I say this because good things can reach perfection, which we obtain by learning from the mistakes we make during the process.

If you are a teacher, salesperson, businessman, manager, pastor, or any other professional, you must know that equilibrium in life is the key that unleashes our living well and our personal growth. Jim Rhon, businessman and great motivational speaker who became a millionaire at 31 years of age, said in one of his conferences that what causes people to fulfill their purpose in life, "is not the wind that blows, but the direction of the boat." What Jim was referring to with that phrase is to circumstances, possibilities and difficulties.

We live in a world in which we can't pretend that we won't have difficulties, because that is impossible. From the time you get up in the morning until you go to bed you face an ocean of difficulties. These have no end. Therefore, the man who succeeds is not measured by the difficulties he avoids, but by the ones he faces.

To avoid problems for fear of failure is the first characteristic of the person who is not heading toward success. When I was the Director of Publications in the Education, Home and Health Service in my country, I was in charge of two young ladies who never did what they were asked to do. They never reached the goals, even though the other coworkers did.

One day, I started to take interest in them and to observe to see what was the reason for their poor performance. So I asked them what was happening, and they answered that I had been unfair, because I had assigned them a place where there were only poor people, which was why their performance was so poor. But the young ladies didn't know that that had been the same place where Sandra — today my wife — and I had worked. It was there where we became champions of summer sales, which had allowed us to get two scholarships to study and it allowed me to obtain the position of general champion of sales. From that position I became associate director of the region of Cibao, in the Dominican Republic. So I smiled and told them, "Oh ... does that mean that I am the one to blame for your failures?"

Most people have two false reasons for not achieving what they want. First, they claim that circumstances are not in their favor. Second, they claim that someone was against them and that's why it was impossible to achieve their goal. But if you are one of those people who always have reasons to justify yourself, remember that the world gives the same opportunities and the same setbacks to all.

The world consists of opportunities and difficulties; it has always been that way and will always be that way. After abundance comes recession, after the storm comes the calm; it's simple, that's it; opportunities after difficulties. Winds blow for all in the same way. Political winds, economic winds, social winds. The key is not to let yourself be carried away by them. The key is to assign a point of arrival to your sailboat. If the wind determined where the sailboat goes, all of them would get to the same port.

But things are not that way. People want things to change, but they want to make that happen by asking for the difficulties to change as well. Nevertheless, the key is not to change the difficulties; we are the ones who need to change. Wanting the boss to change is not a great idea, neither will it give you a better salary. Change yourself, and with that, your world and your circumstances will change. Once I heard the following phrase: "There are no big problems, only small minds." I meditated on it, until I reached the conclusion that the phrase is right, but I also thought of something better. This is the phrase that I like the most and it has become my own philosophy of life: "There are no big problems, only small faith." Faith can move mountains and reach the unreachable.

Change yourself, and with that, your world and your circumstances will change.

When the two young ladies told me that they were not

doing what was asked of them because I had assigned them a bad territory, I told them that the next day I was going out with them and that I was sure we were going to have good results. Of course, they argued that it would be better if I were to change the assigned territory because that one had already been well covered. So the next day I went out with them and, to their surprise, that afternoon we had great results.

The surprising thing was that they had not gone to any of the places where we had good sales, even though they assured me they had gone there. Whenever one of the young people who were under my care gave me reasons for not reaching his goal, I immediately proved to him that he was wrong. But never with theoretical arguments, but instead with evidence, with realities; I would go out with them and make a sale in the exact location where they said it wasn't possible.

Alex Day declares that "reasons are like the navel, everyone has one, but it is not good for anything." *(CD, Yes, you can)* No one becomes a manager or completes a project with arguments, because the people who have achieved success know that circumstances always come our way and affect everyone; the rich, the poor, the good, the bad, whites, Americans, Asians Africans, etc. In every country, in every job, in every home, there are good and bad times.

If you analyze it, you must know that the whole universe is governed by the same natural laws. The sun rises in the morning and sets in the evening. It rains every once in awhile. Days have 24 hours. Weeks have 7 days. Months have 30 or 31 days, and every year has 365 days. The seasons are: spring, summer, fall and winter. Opportunities arise for everyone, and problems as well. What determines your success is not the problems you have, but the way you face them.

It's not a matter of beating on something, but learning how to do it right

There is a story that a man who was driving his Ford had a mishap and the vehicle broke down. As a result of the situation, the man was sweaty and grumpy, when a well-dressed man stopped his car and offered to help. The man accepted, so the stranger lifted the hood of the broken-down car, checked some things and, with one single touch, fixed the engine and the car started running.

The owner of the car was pleasantly surprised and with great admiration asked: "How could you make the car start so easily, since I have been trying to make it work for more than two hours?" The stranger looked at him, stretched out his hand and, with a smile on his face told him: "Pleased to meet you; I am Henry Ford, the one who made this car." He who knew how the car worked, could make it work with one stroke. If you know what you're doing, you will do it well. Find out what it is that people need and when they need it; that way your work will be easier and more effective.

I have discovered that you don't have to lie to convince someone. On the contrary, the more confident you are of what you do, the better you will do it, because preparation is a ladder of many steps, but you always have to take steady and sure steps. There are people who believe that they can grow by deceiving others, but that doesn't turn out well, because no matter how foolish people are, some day they will realize that you are not trustworthy.

Another factor is that many people say that you can achieve what you want by working hard, but that is not true either. Most millionaires have not done hard or heavy jobs. Many of them don't even know what it's like to work an hour of overtime. Why do I say this? Because when people work overtime, they don't have time to organize their thoughts and direct their energies.

Mind and strength divided don't yield good results. Success is not achieved by working hard, but by using well your wisdom and thoughts. Directing your ideas, your work, your thoughts and getting trained in what you want to do is the key for everyone who wants to achieve success in life.

Success is not achieved by working hard, but by using well your wisdom and thoughts.

For years I had the idea that hard work was going to help me in my personal growth. One day I woke up and realized that I was very tired, that my body was not responding, and my organs refused to keep going at the pace I was going. I wanted to do everything and that was giving me a momentary growth, but real growth is obtained through training and a gradual process, because that kind of success doesn't die with you.

The Americans have a saying, "Knowledge is power."

But this saying is not entirely true, because knowledge is power only when we focus it. Otherwise, it is a waste of time. What do I mean by that? I mean that when a person begins to study something that is of no use in what he does, he is only wasting time and losing focus.

Knowledge is power only when we focus it in the right direction. If you are a mechanic, having knowledge about anatomy will not help you grow in your career. If you are a medical doctor, having knowledge about how to travel to space will not increase your profits or efficiency. If you are a machine operator, having knowledge about American History and The Pilgrims will not get you promoted to a better position. So, when you receive training in something that will be a benefit to what you do, no matter what it is, that training will lead to your growth.

Remember this: what makes a person grow is not the occupation he has, but the focus and persistence he has in what he does. Knowing what you're doing is what makes the difference. When you do something, make sure you know well the place where you are going to do it, and why you are going to do it. Doubts don't let you go forward, and ignorance keeps you from doing things effectively. Learn well what you do and you will have no regrets.

In conclusion, what makes a professional is not so much the work he does in itself, but the confidence with which he does it and the training he has to get it done. A salesperson is not just a person who does direct sales; rather, it is every person who lives on this planet. The techniques that are used to sell things work for all of us, in any area that we work, because they give us confidence and training, and above all, they make us more enthusiastic and positive people. I wanted to raise this topic in this book, not only for those who work in sales, but also for those who get up every day with a challenge to overcome.

CHAPTER 8

THE NETWORK MARKETING BUSINESS

In the new game of business, the winners are not the best,
but those who master the game.
Roberto Serra

The world is made up of communities, which have made way for large cities. These, in turn, make up nations. On the other hand, countries have united to deal with the great challenges that they face in the present and will face in the future. Resources are becoming increasingly limited, population growth is increasing and jobs are becoming scarce. That is the perfect setting for the establishment of the phenomenon that we know today as globalization.

Moreover, when we talk about networks, we are referring to the art of association of entities that make an interweave like a net. We will talk about this subject later. Great business figures, such as Robert Kiyosaki and Donald Trump, have said that the network marketing business represents the greatest opportunity for this century. In fact, among the firms that make up the world of network marketing are those of human welfare, those that have to do with health and communication, among other things. These are the best, because it is expected that in the next five years — only in the line of items that improve health — there will be an annual consumption of 10 trillion dollars. That deserves to be analyzed — of course, only if you happen to be one of those people who are seeking economic growth.

Now, there is the class of very wealthy people. And even though they, the baby boomers — those who were born after the Second World War — have been a generation famous for its lifestyle, they are already in decline, in the final stages of their existence. And since they are the type of people who have economic means, they love to live well. So, they are potential candidates to consume products that improve their health and provide them greater comfort.

However, every generation is better than the previous one, since the children outperform the parents. And, of course, it is expected that children will achieve more things than their parents, which makes the parents rightly happy. My parents, for instance, were born in the countryside and they were farmers in the Dominican Republic. One day, my father sold everything he had there and moved to the city to prepare the way for us so that we would not be farmers like them.

He hoped his children could go to school and learn in order to have a better life. Today, I live in New York, and my children are American citizens, go to American schools, and they can learn another culture and another world. I, however, have my limitations in this regard, but I am very happy that they can improve their daily lives. In fact, I hope my kids surpass me in everything. That is not going to be a disgrace for me; on the contrary, it will be an honor.

My parents also feel honored that today I am a way for them to enjoy a better life. They did what they could and I am very grateful to them. Now, I have to do my best so my kids can be grateful to me, although that is not why I do it. With all this, what I want you to learn is that, when you make a good decision, you are not only sowing just for you, but also for the generations to come. Quite probably they will be much more benefited than you are, because many of the things that you want to do and see, time and circumstances will not allow you to complete, but your offspring will see them, and that's what's important.

> *When you make a good decision, you are not only sowing just for you, but also for the generations to come.*

Network marketing businesses offer you a better future

People have many concerns about the future and that is valid, as long as they do it in a healthy way and under a natural degree of faith and trust. We all have concerns about how we are going to live, if we are going to own a house for our children; about the quantity of resources that we are going to have or receive the day we no longer have strength to work anymore, etc. These concerns become a powerful force to make us move forward and rise up to new challenges.

One of the great blessings that network marketing offers us is that in our old age we can count on the results that this business gives us, and our children can also benefit from it. These companies are designed to help people to build a business without resources and without much effort. It's like planting a tree. You plant it, you take care of it and wait for the results: the fruits.

One of the greatest challenges that this generation faces is to learn to wait. We have to learn to undergo the process of life because it is in constant development and evolution. I don't believe in the Theory of Evolution or anything that denies the existence of God as the Creator;

but I agree that things were made to evolve, because nothing was made finished. Everything was made to undergo transformation, to evolve, to develop and grow. God could have given men a world with skyscrapers, communication systems and everything done well and ready. But He only did it with the necessary resources to go through the process of transformation to see the evolution of all things.

Now, networks can't be built in a day and that can drive some people crazy, especially those who believe that things are going to fall from heaven. Networks grow little by little, like a baby who is born, a plant that is planted, the student who enrolls in school, etc. There is a logical process that must be followed.

What is important to know

When someone is going to work in a network marketing business, she or he has to take into consideration that there are many and there's a wide variety. All offer unlimited opportunities for advancement, and that is important, but it is very important that before you start your business, you stop and analyze carefully which one fits your personality best. I have seen people who start doing business and fail to get rolling for years, but, because they persist, they have become successful people.

I also have seen those who have switched companies, and by doing so, they have become successful people. The only problem is that many people think that the key to their success was changing companies, but that is not true. What am I saying? I am saying that there are some things we like more than others. There is nothing wrong with that. When the system and the product of one company does not fit my personality, that is, my ethics, my lifestyle, or what I actually want to do, that will make it difficult for me to achieve success.

The key to growth in a job is that you feel comfortable, that you are certain that this is the one for you. Why? Because there are many companies, but only one "you." Failure is not caused by the company where you work or serve; failure is caused by you, because all the network marketing businesses are made for people to succeed. Besides, they don't gain anything when people fail.

The other important thing is that if you have doubts, if you are not sure that you are in the right place and doing the right thing, the moment you see other offers, you are going to get confused, you are going to leave what you are doing and you will not achieve the success you desire. Many people have lost their credibility in this type of business because every time they see something new, they go for it, and so they go from company to company. With that attitude, the only thing they do is lose credibility, faith, and strength. This principle fits any person, any career, any occupation, anything.

When I was in school, my first and second grade teacher, with whom I learned my first philosophy of life, told me: "A drip that always hits the same spot can make a hole, even if the target is a rock." One day, the teacher took me to one of the classrooms, showed me how some small ants had made a hole in the concrete floor, pointed to the hole and told me: "Wilson, this is the power of persistence." The lesson I learned was that neither the size of your goals nor your qualities matter when there is persistence in achieving a goal. Goals are what make the difference; they change your future, your achievements.

> *Goals are what make the difference; they change your future, your achievements.*

Partnership is a power with which the impossible is achieved

The power of partnership is an art; it is not easy to do, but he who achieves it has the key and the secret to prosperity. In the Bible, we find a lot about this. Jesus, the Teacher, said: "If two of you shall agree on earth as touching any thing that they shall ask, it shall be done for them of my Father which is in heaven." *(Matthew 18:19 KJV)* The power of the Christian Church was manifested once when 120 of the followers of Jesus were able to be in agreement.

It is said that in ancient times, Noah's descendants, the ones who survived the Flood, got together to make a tower that would reach heaven. That made God organize a meeting in heaven to solve the conflict. Of course, what upset the Creator was the attitude of the hearts of those who were united for a purpose. The conflict was resolved by putting new languages in their mouths, which made it difficult for them to understand their co-workers, thereby dissolving the project. Partnerships, whether for good or for evil, produce results; that is a law. When two people unite and put their hearts on a single purpose, no one can stop them, and they will achieve whatever they want.

The power of network marketing lies in the act of recruiting people to be united in a single purpose. One does not do the business alone; you have to know the power of partnership; the company you belong to teaches you that, and they encourage you to seek others. This is the same principle that Jesus used. The Bible states that He chose twelve and sent them out two by two; later He sent out seventy others two by two. *(Luke 9:1–2; 10:1)* This caused unprecedented results. Partnering has the power to achieve the impossible. How is this achieved? I will show you in just a moment.

Partnering defeats time

People have limited strength and life; we can make many plans, but unless we learn to multiply, these plans will become our enemies. It is normal for a man to work eight hours, sleep eight hours, and use what is left to shower, to eat, to socialize, etc. If a person wants to break this cycle because he needs to produce more, it is likely that he will end up sick or very tired, and, what is worse, abandoning his goals and objectives.

Success in life is not for the people who work more, but for those who have or learn the art of partnership. This is an art when it comes to human beings. In fact, they are the only beings that have this power and the ones who can benefit most from it, but sadly, they are the ones who use it least. When you learn to group people together for a common good, you learn that energy is conserved and you produce more.

No matter how much of a Superman you think you

are, you can't do in eight hours what six people can do in eight hours. If I want to produce without limits, the only thing I have to do is partner without limits. When I do that, I am breaking the limits imposed by time and space.

Partnership implies a common good

I was a pastor of one of the churches that practice partnership the most. Its system is based on a countless number of divisions, which operate together in one single nucleus. But partnership is not effective only when it operates as a union of many people; rather, when the group of people works toward a common good. The union must come from the heart, and give cohesion to the soul, the mind and the body; for this to work, there must be a common purpose; otherwise people will start resisting.

There are two evils that inhibit partnership; they live in the innermost core of men. All humans have them, to a greater or lesser degree. These two evils are envy and selfishness. It is impossible to form a strong partnership when we are envious and selfish people. So, we have to subdue those evils, so that we can have a strong organization; and for that to happen we must think on the well-being of others. The key is: when you grow, I grow; for me to do well, I have to strive for you to do well.

My greatest accomplishment in life is not when I can have a certain amount of money in my bank account, but when I see a person achieve his or her goal. My passion is to motivate people to keep going, encourage them to achieve their goals, and help them to succeed. That should be your passion as well. What makes me most passionate about a person is not the qualities that they have, neither the perfection with which they can do something; but their ability to adapt to the group and work toward a common good. Even when the person has many flaws, to me, he is the right person.

The world tempts you with the idea of finding the perfect person, the ideal man or woman, the talented person, the most qualified; but, although that has its place and should not be criticized, if all this talent is not accompanied by love, service, goodness, integrity, etc., it will not help that much. To be able to unite people, it is necessary that they see that you are thinking about them, that they are important, that they have value, that they are useful for more than being a step in the ladder of success of the person who is directing them. Of course, they can't resist recognizing that that is what they are, but we can't lose human feelings or the human touch. What I mean is that, for my leader to grow, I have to be willing to let him lean on me. However, my mentor also has to understand that in order for me grow, I need to lean on him as well. As the saying goes: "All for one and one for all."

In conclusion, what I'm saying is that partnership has an infinite and unlimited power; it is like the power of God, which is capable of covering the earth. Those who want to grow in anything they do have to recognize the power of networking, the power of reproduction. It is like working without working, like earning without investing, it is being present while you sleep and rest. It is a divine power; it is to be omnipresent, omnipotent, and omniscient. It is conquering time and space. It is a law of God, and all His laws represent His character, which is why they have His very power.

CHAPTER 9

DEVELOP YOUR SKILLS

An average skill, with effort, goes further in any art, than a talent without it.

Baltasar Gracian

When I give a presentation at a seminar or workshop, some people ask me: "What is more important, skills or talent? I tell them that skills are more important. Why? Because they are what we develop with training.

Then, what is a skill? It is the ability to do something with ease, an ability that we acquire through practice. On the other hand, talents are capabilities, gifts that we are born with and that allow us to carry out something with grace.

Although skills allow us to do something well and easily, the difference is that they come by daily practice and through the capacities that have to do with character. It is the skill to perform something, or the capacity to achieve goals through some actions in connection with people. The formation of skills depends on actions, knowledge and habits that make up a non-addictive system containing the skills.

Skills are formed and developed through exercise by constant training, and usually they don't appear in isolation, but integrated into a system. Work with skills assumes the performance of certain actions that allow, in line with the planned objectives, putting into practice the acquired content and the means of carrying out the activity in question. In other words, skills are obtained through our training. Proof of that, is that there are people who have mastered something very well, even though they were not born with that skill.

Once, a fan told a piano teacher:

"You are a genius!"

"Why do you say that?" the teacher asked.

"Because you play the piano with a facility that could only be shown by a super-gifted person.

The piano teacher looked at him and added:

"If practicing 18 hours a day, every day of my life for 20 years is being a genius, then, I am one.

That is what I called skill, something that comes through daily work, with constant practice, with hard work. On a path like this, no one can go wrong.

When I was in high school, I observed many students who had the capability of having fun: they had one or two girlfriends each year, they would go from one night club to another, work, go out on vacations, miss school some days, not take notes during class, but in spite of that, they got good grades and advanced to the next level.

One day I took an interest in that subject, since this is how it was for one of my fellow students, whom they called Mayimbe (a word used to refer to someone who has all the advantages). So I asked him what he was doing to live that way. He answered that all he had to do was to listen to something, or take a quick look at it, and everything was recorded in his mind.

What a contrast to my experience! I had to read things over and over, ask God to give me a vision in the night and make some additional effort or another to retain the information in my mind. But the difference between that young man and me was that he had a talent that I didn't have. Even so, I always got better grades than the gifted guy. And that was because I worked harder than he did. The reason for success is not the gifts with which we are born, but the skills we develop; these skills are more important than everything else.

The reason for success is not the gifts with which we are born, but the skills we develop; these skills are more important than everything else.

Recruiting skills

Attracting people to join your vision is an art, but one that will take you to the highest peak. I have seen many people who have difficulty getting people to follow them. To do that, you need leadership, and every person who can make another follow him is already a leader. A leader is a person who can make someone follow him, who can persuade another and involve him in his vision. Later on we will look at more details about this topic, but now I want to tell you that recruiting people is a skill, and it can be learned and developed. When a person fails to get people to follow him, it means that he is not preparing himself to do what he does.

The first time I was chosen to be a leader, it was in the Department of Education, Home and Health, in the Dominican Republic. Immediately I started to notice that many people who had been working there longer didn't like the idea. They doubted my abilities and they refused to follow me. So then I had to start working with a group of inexperienced people, and some, although they stayed, would go every day to the office of my superiors to lodge complaints about me.

That made me realize that I had to work harder than all those who worked with me, and all the other directors who worked in the other regions. I worked my hours and overtime, and, because I realized that the most expert ones were betting on my downfall — it was so bad that when I tried to help them, they insisted on making it a bad day — I decided to work with the inexperienced people; that was a complete success.

When the rest, those who wanted me to fail, realized that, even when they spoke badly about me to my boss, they were seeing the great work I was doing with the novices, they decided to join me, to ask me for help and to spend time with them; that made me win the respect of my superiors and my coworkers and besides, it made even those with more experience join me. It became easier as time went by, they respected me more and more, and each time it was easier to recruit.

Now, to recruit, all you have to do is tell your story and show your example. Recruiting others is easy as long as people realize that they can trust you, that you know where you are going, that you know what you want, and that they and their refusals will not make you hesitate.

Now, to recruit, all you have to do is tell your story and show your example.

To recruit requires tenacity, perseverance, security,

and above all having a vision and a reason to speak to people. When you present to people what you want for them and for yourself, do it firmly and with assurance. If they say no, tell your inner being: "Having a better life requires much more resistance," and continue with the next person. Don't get discouraged with refusals; they are part of the process. You will not build anything that you don't believe in, nor will you achieve anything if you believe that everyone will be in agreement with you. The only person who has to be in agreement with you is yourself. Win the candidate to recruit with sound arguments. Finally, extend an invitation to the potential recruit and continue to speak to others about your dreams.

The ability to sell

I have already spoken about salespeople and about the importance of this profession. Now, sales themselves are very important, because in a world with so much competition, the first thing we need to know how to market is ourselves.

Sales, like recruitment, do not only need the disposition of the individual; they also require constant training and ongoing instruction. Although many companies don't like to talk about sales, mistakenly believing that if they tell people they have to sell something, they will run away, with the experience I have, I can tell you that those who know about sales and are trained to sell are the ones who have more opportunities in life.

When a person comes to any company and is trained to do sales, he will be more qualified to advance in any other responsibility assigned to him. The time people spend working in sales is a time of preparation, because to have success in this field it is necessary to know the product well and to know the psychology of people's behavior.

I have heard many people in multilevel or network marketing companies who claim that their business is not a sales business. I am not against that philosophy if that is used to calm the fears of the new people who are interested, but in reality, every company that is not a sales company and yet produces money is illegal. For a business to be legal, it has to have a product and that product needs to be sold, because, of course, that product cannot be given away free.

There are people who don't manage to take off in their networking business until after two years. Why? Because during that time they are being trained in the thing they don't want to admit they are doing: sales. Can you imagine that you start a business and you don't want to sell, and instead of selling, you consume the product to support yourself? That behavior not only will put the brakes on your aspirations, but it will make the process longer and more tedious, because if you consume the product instead of giving it to others to consume, you are taking from them the opportunity to be united with you.

This principle can be applied to everything we do, whether in church, in a company, in a business and even in the realm of our ideas. Everything must first be absorbed by us to be able to convince others, but if we fill ourselves and we are convinced of what we want to do without imparting it others, we will get stagnated and will not obtain the growth we need. Consuming the product is very important, because it gives you the opportunity to know the product and the assurance that what you are offering to others is good, but selling it to others is what is going to make you grow and develop your business.

It is very possible that at first you are not willing to sell full time, or you may not want to make a living out of it. That is a very valid attitude, but refusing to sell the product even part time is unforgivable, and will not help you to achieve what you want. My experience is that most people who enter a company and then start doing the business, do it because they tested the product and it gave positive results.

Perhaps just presenting a business opportunity to a person that can make him a millionaire will not excite him, but presenting to him a product that can solve his immediate problem as well as that of others could move him to do something. In other words, both to sell and to recruit is to go step by step, one step at a time; one word at a time, one concept at a time. Not everyone learns everything in one day, but we can all learn; it is a matter of practice. The key is: "Try, fail, and try again." *(Alex Day)*

Selling is the key to recruiting. Those who are experts in sales will do well in recruiting, as long as they don't focus on sales only. You may be saying: "But I don't have a product to sell." However, you still have something, for instance, you may have an idea. We have already said that we will always have something to sell, even if it's our personality.

The advantage of networking businesses, just like any other occupation that has to do with people, is that even though there is a product to sell, the business offers you the opportunity to move up and advance in the future, without having to make sales, and without having to recruit anyone, by advancing to something better: training.

Training skills

It is quite possible that you don't have the ability to train others, but this, like all other skills, can be developed and obtained through education and time.

To be able to grow we have to follow the following method: learn, teach, train others and send. It's that easy. If people are not trained, they don't reproduce, and if they don't reproduce, they don't grow; those who enter any discipline and don't reproduce, get stuck and soon will abandon the activity. That applies to everything we do. If there is something that can make us grow, like doing a job or practicing a discipline, and it doesn't produce any change in us after ten years, two things must be happening: 1) either you haven't worked efficiently; 2) or that thing, in reality, doesn't offer the appropriate development.

When a business, a church, a company, offers you suitable growth, it will be noticed as the time goes by. A decade is an appropriate lapse of time for noticing growth, since even one is a complete life, and he who doesn't train for that will soon disappear. The reason for this is that he who is growing will not stop to wait for someone who isn't growing. Constant training is the only thing that will allow you to have solid and gradual growth; it will also help you multiply your philosophy and to have better results.

I have noticed that the people who come to a place displaying a self-sufficient attitude, those who refuse the learning process and to be under authority; those who come questioning leaders, rarely get the results they were expecting, which is why they soon disappear. A humble and submissive attitude in the new disciple will make the training easier, it will make it more effective and growth will be more certain.

People who come to a place displaying a self-sufficient attitude ... rarely get the results they hoped for.

Remember that the system is already made; success belongs to you, but there is something that nothing and no one can change: your attitude. No one can modify it. Besides, life is a two-way road: one way is called learning and the other is called teaching. It is simple: learn, teach, and send. This is the key to success.

Leadership skills

When I was little, I would get up early every Sunday morning to exercise in a youth organization called Medical Cadets. There I learned first aid, among other important skills. There was a phrase that impressed me greatly; it was the motto of the group, and we would sing it while we were training by doing double time marching and jogging.

The phrase went like this: "Cadets are not born, they are made; the possible is already done and we will do the impossible, Sir." We would repeat it again and again during our entire training. The point here is: Is the leader born or made? To me —and you don't have to agree with me— the leader is born as well as made. But the person who is a born leader, has innate leadership qualities. His temperament is like that of a leader, his personality, and his mental alertness. Many people may even be born into a position in which being a leader is their destiny, but the true leader isn't the one who is born with those qualities, but he who makes them work, he who strives to cultivate them, he who spends time on them each day, until he achieves the impossible and overcomes his limitations.

I have always liked leadership, but I have not always been the leader I wanted to be. The reason for that is because I was born and raised with many limitations. Shyness, low self-esteem, and little fluency in the language have been some of the "giants" that I have had to face, but all my life — wherever I have been — I have had leadership roles, since I was in first grade.

People always saw something in me that I was unable to see. That has been my struggle, to know who I am and what I am capable of doing. To form a leader, one has to be able to see what that person is unable to see. For a leader to be born, that person must be able to see himself as a leader. Here there's no place for modesty or the alleged humility of the one who thinks himself unworthy and therefore sees nothing.

For a leader to be born, that person must be able to see himself as a leader.

On the other hand, I have always liked to make other leaders stand out. Sometimes I even got myself into arguments defending people whom I didn't even know. Although that appeared to be something good, it would show something about me, my insecurity about thinking myself qualified. I would discredit myself and give credit to anyone who was nearby or someone I had just seen on television or another setting.

That is why I thank those who always inspired me, those who have looked me in the eye and told me: "God wants to do something big with you." It is interesting how self-esteem works, and how it affects leadership. Most of the people in positions of leadership who use that position to humiliate others instead of to bless them, do so because they are not sure of themselves. Your leadership will start when you begin to be confident about yourself.

In my youth, I always wore sunglasses, even on the darkest nights. I was bashful about people looking me in the eyes; I thought they were ugly and I was going to scare the girls. One very dark night, I was talking with my friends and, as always, I had my sunglasses on. As if by magic, I saw a beautiful blonde walking toward me, and I didn't have the courage to look her in the eye. She always came to the place where I worked and tried to make me smile, but to get a smile out of me was very difficult. I hid behind a facade. I believed that my sullen face would make people respect me. I hardly laughed.

That night the young lady was an inch away from me. I could feel her breath, which disturbed my mind. I could not think; she was so close that I didn't speak anymore, and I tried to react as I almost always did, hurting people with harsh words, especially females. I remember one day when I was in high school a young lady touched me. It bothered me so much that I threatened to throw her down the stairs and my friends had to intervene. When I was a child I was raped by an adult young woman who threatened to tell everything to my mom unless I continued satisfying her passions. That situation made me hate any woman, once I had intimacy with her. That situation left such a mark on me that God had to work with me for many years, with different processes, until finally — in a retreat — I was completely healed. As a general rule, people who have been hurt have the tendency to hurt others.

Going back to the blonde of my story, she approached me and didn't give me the chance to move away; she put her body next to mine in a brazen way, took off my sunglasses, looked me in the eye and, with a smile, told me: "You have beautiful eyes, has anyone told you? Why don't you take off those sunglasses and let others see them?"

I mumbled something trying to say a word, but before I did it she planted a kiss on my mouth and with a brazen smile she walked away. I never talked to her about that incident, although I saw her again many times. But that made me take off my sunglasses and let other people see my eyes. That young lady got me to take off my sunglasses, but before taking them off of me, she took away my insecurity. We can't get good results until we find the cause that prevents us from doing it.

Leadership is based on the confidence you have in yourself and in what you do. You can't be a good leader if you don't have self-confidence. Developing good leadership requires everything we have already said, but the only thing that is required to begin the career of leadership is to believe that you have worth, that people value you and what you have to offer. That is necessary for growth.

In conclusion, we need to learn to develop our skills. Many times, insecurity and fear take over, keeping us from logical and gradual growth. You can achieve what you have purposed, even if you don't have the economic resources to do it. Why? Because you have the necessary resources; they are within you; they were given to you as a gift from God before you were born. Being successful is not only having goods and money, it is being a good father, a good friend, a good husband, being happy, and above all, overcoming all your traumas and complexes.

MORE THAN A DREAM is the way to get motivated to be a better person, to search within you and in the world for the resources you need, to pursue your happiness and that of your family. Cultivate this, bring out the best in you, and develop what you have, because that is sufficient for the success you want so much.

CHAPTER 10

STEPS TO OBTAINING GOOD RESULTS

"I can't do it" never accomplished anything;
"I will try" has wrought wonders.
George Burnham

As I have said, we all have reasons for not doing things, but those reasons are not good enough. No one gets an increase in salary for giving his boss a reason for not doing well or not doing something the way he was asked. Reasons are only good for us, not for anyone else.

People get into arguments because they are unable to admit failure; or because they are unable to ask for help; or because they lack humility to recognize that they need to learn or that they haven't prepared well. Therefore, we must be able to admit our limitations and needs, and at the same time learn the first principle of prosperity: to be malleable and allow people to teach us.

In the Bible we see Jesus struggling with this kind of people, those who think they know everything. Many people are that way; they don't want to change their way of thinking. They don't have any arguments or reasons to go on the way they are, disconsolate, sick and unhappy. They are people who don't obtain good results, even when they have everything.

Those who wouldn't allow themselves to be molded, the Master called, "old wineskins"; people who were not willing to see the world differently, those who didn't seek results, but excuses; those who thought they knew everything and no one could teach them. I know many people who are like that, in fact, I was in a place where people think they know everything, that they don't need anything from anyone, that the rest of the world should think like them, otherwise they are wrong. But when I left that environment to go out into the real world, I saw that others were getting better results. The respect due a discipline or a person has nothing to do with what they think or do, but with the results obtained.

Excuses are not good enough. When someone invites me to do some business — one having to do with referrals and to which I can't dedicate enough time — and they insist that I can earn extra money with the referrals, the first thing I make clear is that I can go with him to visit some people, but that I can't commit to them in their company, because I don't have the time to devote and my focus is not on that at that moment.

That prevents two things. This first one is that I don't get myself involved in something that is not my calling. The second one is that the person doesn't have expectations that I am not going to meet; not because I can't, but because I don't want to and because at that moment I am not going to devote enough time to it. When you are not going to do something well, the best thing is not to do it, or make it clear how far you will get. That will make other people trust you more the next time. Your credibility is worth more than your money.

Your credibility is worth more than your money.

Doing something with excellence is your best letter of introduction. It is what qualifies you to be believed in, for that reason I urge you not to waste it, not to sell it, because it is priceless.

One day a young lady presented me a business opportunity. She said I had many talents, which is true, and that the company needed someone like myself. I answered that I was capable of doing it but the problem was that I didn't have enough time to do it with excellence. I explained to her that when I do something, I can't afford to do it wrong.

However, there are people who get involved in something without thinking. That doesn't work; in fact, it is an unforgivable wrong; it is something that unsuccessful people do, and you, a champion, are not one of them. "But I have not been able to do it well," many people say. That may be an excuse, but what I am telling you is that no matter how many reasons or excuses you have, you must change today.

As I write this book, I am going through a process. For nine months I have been living on my savings, and I am not talking about a small budget.

This happened to me because I decided to leave the world I knew — my comfort zone — and move into a new one. I have my reasons for doing this, which is why I am determined to do what I am now considering. It doesn't matter how much it costs. It is my dream. God has put it in my heart, which is why I can't fail to do it.

But, what am I saying? Going through a time of process doesn't make you a loser. Many people only believe in the word of the great millionaires and in what they have already been in a certain company. But there is also credibility for the one who wants to start, for the one who says: "I want to change everything I have done and do something new," for him who wants to change the results.

The great millionaires and the most prominent men you know have something in common: many of them have declared bankruptcy maybe several times. They are who they are because they are not afraid of what others will say. They are not afraid to go further to seek new results, and of course, in that searching you have to learn to lose and to win.

The important thing is not how many times you have lost, but how many times you did your best to win, because when you lose a game, it doesn't mean you have lost the tournament; of course, if you learn how to get the best results.

In my pastoral ministry at the organization where I worked, I always did more than I was asked. When they asked me for one hundred, I did one hundred and one. And that is what happens in all the areas in which I perform. When I have had to work in companies of personal development or sales, I have had the same results. I have broken the records and I have made it to the hall of fame. I have star-studded rings and my walls are full of awards, but that doesn't make me superior to anyone; I have my mistakes and my failures.

That is why, if you are a person with limitations, I invite you to believe in yourself and to stop looking at your excuses and focus on the results. These, ultimately, are what speak for you. And they give you the power to influence others.

Let's see some simple steps to get results with people and to influence others.

Greeting and friendly contact

This is a focal point, it's your first presentation, it's the impression you make the moment other people see you. And it has to do with your personality and skills.

People will treat you depending on how you present yourself. They will give you the importance you think you have. This is a complicated point in a world where some things are not valued, where everything looks good and nothing looks extravagant, where it seems that good manners don't matter to anyone. But that is the problem. People who like what's good and care about what's important, also like to see where those things come from. They will not only see the product, but the one who offers it.

People who like what's good and care about what's important, also like to see where those things come from. They will not only see the product, but the person who offers it.

Friendly contact includes two things: a person's presentation and the presentation of what that person is representing. Both of them have to be well displayed.

The Promoter

When a person promotes or represents something, he will succeed or fail depending on how he does it. A good product should not be presented poorly; a good company must be well-presented, but here I am talking about the image, not the presentation itself. We will talk about that later.

Clothing

This is a key topic. Clothing has to be clean and ironed. I am one of those who think that if you are not going to wear a suit and tie, at least wear a good quality outfit. No one wants to waste their time with a person who doesn't even have the good taste to dress up. The ideal is for the shirt to be white or blue; that gives a sense of honesty and trust to the person who is listening.

Bright colors usually make the person wearing them look dishonest, like someone who only thinks of himself and whose only purpose is to become rich off the other person's resources.

That is why when we deal with a person we don't know, it is recommended that you wear something that reflects transparency and, in addition, is of good quality. Why? Because if the person you visit is going to deposit something of value in your hands, he will not want to give it to anyone.

That applies to all areas, because even when you don't do anything that has to do with money, when it has to do with people, at least it has to do with values.

Once, while I was in training with doctor José Campos, I heard him telling about an experience he had with a new disciple. He went out to teach the new disciple, but they were not received anywhere; on the contrary, when people saw them, it seemed like they were looking at Satan himself. He wondered why, because that rarely happened to him in other cases or with other experiences while training others.

As the veteran that he was, he would not stop going from place to place, trying to teach him the value of perseverance. That was when he decided to go to a house, knocked on the door, and a woman opened it. But immediately, he saw that the woman's face was uptight. Campos asked, "What happened, Ma'am?" And she screamed as if she had seen two ghosts, and immediately closed the door.

José Campos looked at his companion and realized what had happened. The young man had a thick string of snot that hung from his nose and was draped on his tie, and to make matters worse, two big lice were walking on the collar of his shirt as if they were two kids playing at the park.

The first impression says a lot about you. And it also tells if people are going to accept you or not. The same thing happened to me with a young man named Ricardo (this is not his real name, of course). I went out to train him when I was director of publishing, and I noticed that nothing I did was giving me any results. Since nothing was working with the young guy, I wanted to know why, and I discovered that the problem was the poor presentation of the young man. He was wearing a shirt that was hanging out with a tie that came down to mid-chest and one leg of his pants rolled up. Of course, when people saw him, he would look more like a crazy person than a sales representative.

The Smile

We should give our best smile. Learn to smile even if you are not having your best day. And I don't mean splitting your sides, or laughing out loud. It would not be very pleasant if someone were to stand in front of your house or office and when he sees you, he were to burst into laughter. That would seem more like mocking than contentment; or mockery of some defect. What I am referring to is smiling with lips and eyes. These say a lot about you and have a lot of power over others.

I got used to using my eyes to befriend people. I got that ability from more than twenty years I have been working with people, much of that time in sales. Now, I have a problem; oftentimes people from the opposite sex have misunderstood me. How do I know that? My friends have told me. My case is somewhat awkward because I am a pastor and I don't want anyone to misunderstand my friendship. I understand, however, that it is something that comes out naturally — it is part of me. I was trained to do that, and I have practiced it most of the time; my eyes, my smile and my face act at the same time.

At first I had to force myself, then I had to get used to it, but now it is part of my life, and whether misunderstood or not, it is who I am and I can't change it. When you learn a skill, the most interesting thing is that as time goes by, it becomes part of you, to the point where if you want to quit it, you have to try hard. That's why when I talked about habits I mentioned the importance of forming good habits and not bad ones. Smiling makes others feel good, whether they are male or female. Whether you are young or not, it is a good habit that, will open many doors, although many people don't understand this, because people are feeling lack of appreciation.

The way you walk and your posture

People think that walking the way they please is their privilege, but what is important is to know how to do it. You can't do anything good and great, the way the "cornering tigers" do things, even when it is about the Gospel. Why? Because even though people appreciate being accepted just the way they are, when it comes to making a change in their lives, they always prefer something different. No one will be interested in that which does not offer something better than what they already have. Your posture when you knock on a door, when you talk with others, when you stand in front of a door waiting for it to be opened, when you arrive at an office looking for a job, when you talk on the phone with the person who is going to interview you, etc. — all that tells a lot about whether the person involved, and who has to make a decision with you, is going to give you an opportunity or not to be a part of his life and his business.

Friendly contact encompasses everything that has to do with what businessmen called "breaking the ice," opening doors, making friends. So I encourage you, the next time you want to add someone to your vision, to take all that into consideration. It also has to do with sitting down with the person in their house or office, because this not only has to do with who you are, but also with who he is. Highlight his strengths and achievements, look for something good in people, break the ice, make him smile and change his attitude toward you. Praise him and make him feel good, but never disrespect him. The question that comes to your mind is: Isn't that hypocrisy or flattering? No, not at all; making someone feel good is a virtue, not a sin.

The Presentation

Once you have earned the trust of the people, proceed with what you have to do with them. Let them know what you are offering and why you are at their house or office. The presentation encompasses everything we do, not only selling. It is also important when we want to recruit or disciple someone in any discipline or profession that we choose to develop. We have to do this even when we look for a job. We can't let people assume things; we have the responsibility of offering our opportunities to others, and I am not talking about business only, but about all good things that come to our life.

An effective presentation encompasses your philosophy of life, what you are and how you think. Some people only think about how to get benefit from others; everything they do is for that purpose. If you are that kind of person, begin to change. We get more from people when we are authentic, when we give our best to make them better. I started doing professional sales when I was only 14 years old. However, when I became independent, I discovered that there wasn't anything in me that enjoyed making other people stand out, seeing the best in other people. As I pointed out, I was rude with people because I grew up fighting every day in school, and it was hard for me to get anything unless I fought for it. Being courteous with others, telling the secretaries that they looked nice and were efficient, was not my thing; I couldn't do it.

In spite of my ignorance, there is a principle in the art of skills development that I have not discussed so far; it is that whatever you're going to develop, first you have to plant it in your heart, otherwise you will have a hard time succeeding. There must be a purpose and a great desire to succeed, to overcome your limitations and be the person that God wants you to be. If you heart is not in what you do, give it up.

Whatever you're going to develop, first you have to plant it in your heart.

I decided not to quit, because I discovered what many people don't know, that the heart can be changed, that skills can be developed. What made me change? The times I failed, and the need I had for everything to change, to be able to study in a university. But, what did I do? That I will tell you in more detail in my next book that I am already writing. Now, I insisted and asked God with all my heart. I asked Him to help me to love people, to be sensitive to their needs, to want them to feel good when they were with me, and in a natural way, without any pressure, and I succeeded. Something died within me and made way for the birth of another man. It was a long process, but the results were so good that today, the easiest thing for me is to love people and work with them. I can do that without getting paid.

However, let's get back to the topic of the presentation. You are probably thinking: What does this have to do with that? What I am trying to say is that for a long time people will not buy anything from you if you are not original, and it will be even worse if you tell lies. Good preparation and a sense of vocation will help you in your growth and in what you do. As I went out every summer to sell books in order to go to school, the job became easier and easier. Why? Well, because I would make many friends, who would welcome me back every summer, who wanted to buy everything I would show them. The same thing happened in the area of Christianity and ministry. I've always had people who have supported me in all the projects I have presented to them, just because they believe in me.

What makes people interested in your ventures? Besides the affection, love or friendship that they have for you, what makes them interested in you is the security they feel because they know you and what you are presenting to them. This is the most important thing. In addition, you also know your product, and you know how to present it and sell it. Many people fail when they start a new career because they don't prepare. It is impossible to give a good presentation with a bad preparation; this applies to the physical and the intellectual. The same is true even in the spiritual world. Pastoring a church and working with Christians is the same thing. Some pastors can win everyone they see, while others spend their entire life trying to win themselves. This contains a common truth, which is that some people get prepared and others don't even try. Testimonies are good, it is good to have interesting stories to tell, but good preparation is better. Why? Because when we run out of stories to tell, we are still prepared.

It is impossible to give a good presentation with
a poor preparation.

The presentation must be done with preparation and confidence, but the problem is that no one can be sure of what they do not know, much less, present well what they haven't mastered. In order for something to turn out well and be a success, you have to let it touch your heart and run through your veins. Everything that you present with that passion, whether business or beliefs, you will do well and you will have success.

The Conclusion

This step has to do with settling on an end to what we want to do and what we are presenting. In fact, if you want to be successful with all the people you talk to, you have to tell them how long the presentation is going to be, and what's most important, stick to it. What drives people crazy is not knowing how long they have to listen to someone. This could negatively affect the achievement of your goals.

In this step you have to make clear what you want to tell your client, or the potential recruit, if you want the individual to make a decision in favor of what you are presenting.

I learned something that I want to share with you; more than words, they are principles that will bring success when you are talking to a person: "Tell him what you have to say" (Introduction). "Tell him what you are saying" (Presentation) and "Tell him what you said" (Conclusion), that is, go back and refresh the memory of the listener and define the points you have expressed, because by doing that you will clarify his questions and avoid future objections.

Conclude with a calm voice and control of the situation. Give no indication that you don't know what you are talking about or where you are going. One of the big problems of some people who give presentations in the attempt to lead others to make an immediate decision, is that they create gaps that not even they can overcome. Others climb onto such a high pedestal, that later they don't know how to get down. They present the company, the product, and themselves in such lofty terms, that later they have a hard time coming down to earth and reaching a conclusion. While it is true that you ought to do everything with dignity, it is also true that dignity has nothing to do with leaving your audience confused or not understanding your intentions.

That would be like what happens with a young man who falls in love with a young lady. Although he sees her every day, gives her flowers and talks to her, he never tells her anything to confirm what she thinks is happening. That causes her to become disenchanted and she begins to avoid chatting and going out with the guy, and, if a better prospect comes along, it will be over for the undecided guy. Not coming to a good conclusion or making the objective very clear, is like leaving a door open that later you might not be able to close.

Not coming to a good conclusion or making the objective very clear, is leaving a door open that later you might not be able to close.

Let's look at an example.

If someone comes to my office and tells me that he wants to present to me a good program to help families, immediately I will think that he is a salesperson; that would seem most reasonable. But imagine that I take interest in what he wants to present, thinking that if I like something, I may acquire it. There is already a possibility open in my mind. But then, the presenter starts talking about social problems, the alarming criminal cases of the day, and continues with such a long-winded speech that I end up believing he is a preacher.

Then he tells me that families need more and better protection, more financial education, and a guarantee of living better. Now I start believing that he works for the government and that he's likely to offer me a plan for social assistance. But then he opens a folder and shows me several things from which I can benefit. Suddenly, he seems to change his mind and he starts saying that he wants to recruit me or he offers me some kind of benefit, blah, blah, blah. None of that is bad, as long as we can come down to earth from that bubble so we can get to our real goals, because otherwise we, the listener and the presenter, will waste our time.

Here is where the conclusion comes in. In this step, everything that has been said should be clarified and the information should be repeated, because it is possible that at some point in your presentation the person has a mental block and doesn't hear well what you are trying to say. So, in the conclusion, make everything very clear and take it to the next step: The Close.

The Close

As I have already said, the first time I went out to try to sell something, it was books; and as difficult as it is to sell a book in a country where most people think that books are good for nothing, this is not a very promising profession. In fact, most people who do that kind of job are South Americans. Natives, or Creoles, as we say, 95% of the time do not succeed, like myself, who didn't have success in anything that had to do with convincing people. But those who recruited me for this job made me learn a sales talk of ten pages, without the sampler set or any other kind of help. In my head I only had theory.

When it was time to go out in the field, they gave me the sampler set, which had a price; they gave it to me because they wanted to make sure I was really going out in the field and thus would be able to buy it. They did not give that sampler set before going out to the field, because many people would register, but never come back, because they would have thrown it out and there was no way to get the money to pay for it. The thing is that I had to learn the whole sales talk, but I didn't know anything about the sampler set, which consisted of a set of books with a lot of graphics, illustrations, and the best parts of the books you wanted to sell.

The first day people would look at me and smile, many people even congratulated me, the problem was that I was not selling anything to anybody. Then I began to analyze the phenomenon, and I discovered that even though I was giving the sales talk very well, nothing that was coming out of my mouth had anything to do with what I was presenting in the sampler set. It was like a movie where the voices didn't match with the movements of the lips of those who were talking; that is, it was out of sync.

Later, when I learned to combine one thing with the other, I realized that the close of the presentation should not be left to the last, but it is done step by step, at every opportunity one has. The close is not the last thing, although the results are seen at the end. It is something we have to work on from the moment we arrive to see the person, from the moment we sit down with her and utter the first words. All these actions must be aligned with the results we want to obtain. In fact, I discovered that before entering an office to present something to someone, there were details I had to think about if I wanted to have an effective close.

Many people settled with an "almost," "you almost convince me" or with "I will call you later." Some say, "I will think about it," or " I really liked it; believe me, I will do it later," etc. In 99% of the cases, quite simply, the candidate was not satisfied with the information provided.

In my experience, 99% of the people that have made a decision about what I was offering them, first, they told me no, that they would think about it, that the husband wasn't there, that there was no money, that they were not sure, that they were going to call me; yet, I succeeded with all of them. And I know that that is because I was well-prepared and carried out to perfection every one of the steps for obtaining results. He who prepares well and fully carries out every one of the steps for obtaining results, doesn't settle for excuses, but only for results. These are what motivates a successful man. When a person has greatness in mind, he doesn't settle for less.

Those who think about success only settle for results

Recently I made a decision that made many people think that it was beyond insanity. I started a project and for many reasons, down the road, God put in my heart the need of something different from what I knew and was accustomed to doing. I had already started it, but now I had to make fundamental changes to accomplish what I had in my heart. I say this because for a person to get what he wants and have the results he desires, he has to put himself in the road that will lead to that place.

Due to the changes I made, many people were upset. Ninety percent of those who supported me left me, and I had to keep going with some new folks who began to arrive. After three months of prayer and struggle, God gave me this word: "Knock everything down and start again." I didn't want to accept that reality. "Why?" I protested to the Lord, "there is money in the bank account, and new people are arriving." Then I understood why. We were not trained. Although I had worked in something similar for more than 17 years, this was different. We would not be able to do it well if I and those with me now were not trained to get the results we were wanting.

Perhaps we would have gotten results, but not the results we wanted. Many people stay in a similar situation and spend twenty years with the same struggle. Admitting that we need to improve, and that there are people who have done what we want to do, doesn't mean we're weak, it means we are humble and strong. Of course, I didn't give up what God had put in my heart or my dreams; I just joined someone who had a heart like mine, so that what I don't have in terms of training and experience is complemented with what he has. He has what I am looking for and that is enough. That is why, when you wish to get results, there are two things that you should consider. The first is whether you have the resources that you need to do it. The second is whether you have enough training to achieve it.

For instance, to have a franchise from McDonalds, you not only need to have a million dollars, you also have to go for six months to their university to learn their system. They know that if the person doesn't know what he is doing, he is not going to have good results. That is why it is necessary to have both things: resources and training. If you lack one of those two things, be humble enough to admit it and let someone who has what you are looking for, help you; even if you lose something, it is your cost. Many people dream of having their own brand name. Others fail because they are interested in doing something else with their brand name, in their own way, than obtaining good results. To me, the results are more important.

Conclusion

In this work I have tried to detail some of the ingredients that you need to achieve your dream, because More Than a Dream is the key to the secret.

Everybody has dreams. Most people have dreams that don't go beyond their mind; that is to say, they never take shape. They never materialize or become reality. These people live in a dream and don't realize that they are in a real world that they need to face. Things don't become reality just by wanting them, but by working hard and getting trained to obtain them.

All this information that you have received will help you, only if you dare to take it with you, to get it out of your mind and to bring it to the natural world; otherwise it will not work. Dare to use the information that was presented in this book and I assure you that your tomorrow will not be the same.

In today's world there is a lot of information that makes you feel good, but does not necessarily help you to be transformed. That is why I wrote all this material — material that has been reality in my life; information that has overcome the test of fire, because I have literally had to get burned to succeed.

This book is for those who are aware of the value of transformation. The power of change lies in the information that is put into practice, that becomes life. To do otherwise is to waste our time and money. What I have explained here are principles that need to be put into action in order to fulfill the statements, words, and positive thoughts, all of which are very important things, but if they are not carried into action, they will not give results.

About the author

Wilson Santos was born in the city of Cotui, in the Dominican Republic, where he graduated in Theology, Education and Psychology at the UNAD (Dominican Adventist University).

He has been the speaker at multiple conferences and at different businesses, companies, churches and community centers. Also, he is the founder of the Evangelistic Ministry of Radio and Television, "The Power of the Gospel," which has been broadcast on the main radio stations and television channels of New York City; for instance, it has been broadcast on Telemundo, one of the main Hispanic channels and part of the television network ANBC.

In the Dominican Republic, he was Associate Director in the region of Cibao (north, northeast and northwest) of the Service of Education, Home and Health, an institution in charge of recruiting and training young people so that, through sales of educational books, they could win scholarships to study at the university. In the Northwest Mission (SDA) he was a pastor, director of communications, education and publications.

His passion is preaching, motivation and sales, and, through his words and the power of the Creator, he has helped millions of people to change their vision and see hope in the midst a world with so many setbacks.

Through his talks, throughout nearly all the United States, the Dominican Republic and Puerto Rico, as well as his programs on radio and television, he has had multiple experiences of people who have been transformed in a moment — when all seems lost — and where they have been rescued by a single word inspired by the Creator and filled with His power.

Wilson Santos lives in New York City with his wife Sandra and his three children: Wesser, Wesserline and Melody. At present he serves as a conference speaker and promotes his project of personal growth, **MORE THAN A DREAM**. Also, he and his wife Sandra are the main pastors and founders of the Central Church of New York.

For orders, lectures, seminars or exhibits, send an email to: wilsonsantos73@hotmail.com